CONTENTS

Chapter One: The Ethical Debate

Chapter Two: The Medical Debate

First published by Independence
The Studio, High Green
Great Shelford
Cambridge CB22 5EG
England

© Independence 2008

British Library Cataloguing in Publication Data
Euthanasia and the Right to Die – (Issues Series)
I. Firth, Lisa II. Series
179.7

ISBN 978 1 86168 439 4

Printed in Great Britain
MWL Print Group Ltd

Cover
The illustration on the front cover is by
Don Hatcher.

Euthanasia

Information from NHS Direct

Introduction

Euthanasia is against the law in the UK. It is illegal to aid someone to take their life under any circumstances. 'Assisted suicide' or voluntary euthanasia can result in a prison sentence of up to 14 years.

There are religious, moral, ethical and practical arguments surrounding the issue of euthanasia. It is an extremely emotive and controversial subject and has been at the centre of public debate for many years.

Definition

Euthanasia has been defined as:

'The act of killing a person who is suffering from a distressing mental or physical condition';

'when a doctor, friend or relative intentionally ends a person's life, to "put them out of their misery"';

'Compassion-motivated, deliberate, rapid and painless termination of the life of someone afflicted with an incurable and progressive disease'.

However, there is no legal definition of euthanasia, because it is not recognised by British law. It is defined by intent; that is, when one person intentionally facilitates the death of another person.

Voluntary euthanasia (also known as 'assisted suicide')

This is when a person with a terminal (or serious and progressive) illness asks for their life to be ended by a doctor or carer (including a friend or family member). However, if the person with the illness is not considered mentally competent to make decisions about their treatment, it could be seen as murder.

Involuntary euthanasia

This is when a person's life is ended, without their consent, although they are competent and able to make decisions about their treatment. Legally, this is murder.

Non-voluntary euthanasia (also known as 'mercy killing')

This refers to a person's life being ended when they are unable to make decisions regarding their treatment, for example they are in a coma.

There is a distinction between active and passive euthanasia: actively causing a person to die (for example by giving them an overdose) or passively allowing them to die (for example by withdrawing or withholding their treatment).

Policy guidelines

The World Medical Association (WMA) declared euthanasia unethical in 1950.

Euthanasia is against the law in the UK. It is illegal to aid someone to take their life under any circumstances. 'Assisted suicide' or voluntary euthanasia can result in a prison sentence of up to 14 years.

The British Medical Association (BMA) has clear policy opposing euthanasia. It accepts that patients can refuse life-prolonging treatment and that medication designed to keep them comfortable and pain-free may reduce their lifespan. However, it opposes plans to change the law to allow interventions that are intended to end life, such as a lethal injection.

By law, doctors are able to give patients large quantities of drugs to reduce pain or suffering, even if this speeds up death. However, they are not allowed to give drugs with the intention of causing or speeding up death. This is called the doctrine of double effect.

A draft bill called the Patient (Assisted Dying) Bill is being considered by parliament. If this bill is passed, it will 'enable a competent adult who is suffering unbearably as a result of a terminal (or a serious and progressive) illness to receive medical help to die at his own considered and persistent request'.

Getting help

Options available to patients living with a terminal or serious and progressive illness include:

Palliative care

Palliative care is 'treatment of symptoms where cure is no longer

considered an option'; in other words, the patient is dying. It focuses on controlling pain and other symptoms, improving quality of life for the patient and their family, and social, emotional and spiritual needs. Hospices, good medical and nursing care, company, therapy and counselling can all help terminally ill patients. It is argued that if the patient is comfortable, has company, and is not experiencing suffering or pain, they are less likely to consider the route of euthanasia.

Refusing treatment

A patient is not under any legal obligation to accept treatment recommended by a doctor or other healthcare professional. They may refuse treatment at any time, provided they have been properly informed of the consequences and they are 'of sound mind'.

'Assisted suicide' or voluntary euthanasia can result in a prison sentence of up to 14 years

---

The Department of Health guidelines state that:

'Competent adult patients are entitled to refuse treatment, even where it would clearly benefit their health.'

In other words, you have the right to refuse or stop treatment at any time, even if this means that you may die. The exceptions to this rule are patients detained under the Mental Health Act 1983 and children under 18.

Department of Health guidelines state that no one can give consent on behalf of an incompetent adult (for example, a patient who is in a coma). However, healthcare professionals take into account the patient's best interests when deciding on treatment. These 'best interests' are based on:
⇨ the wishes of the patient when they were competent;
⇨ the patient's general well-being; and
⇨ their spiritual and religious welfare.

If a patient is declared clinically brain dead, the decision may be taken to turn off their life support machine. This will be discussed with the patient's family, but the ultimate decision rests with the consultant. Strict criteria must be met when declaring a patient clinically brain dead.

Advance directive (or 'living will')

If you are worried that you may not be able to make your wishes known in the later stages of an illness you may wish to draw up a written document called an advance directive or 'living will'. In this document you can state what you want to happen if you become too ill to decline or consent to medical treatment. An example of this is if you were previously resuscitated in hospital but do not want to be resuscitated again.

An advance directive is legally binding in the UK and will be respected by healthcare professionals. It is recommended that you inform your GP and your next of kin if you make an advance directive, as they may be the first point of contact if you require medical attention.

Glossary

Abortion
An abortion or termination is a medical procedure that ends pregnancy. The method used depends on the stage of pregnancy.

Brain
The brain controls thought, memory and emotion. It sends messages to the body controlling movement, speech and senses.

Coma
A coma is a sleep-like state when someone is unconscious for a long period of time.

Counselling
Counselling is guided discussion with an independent trained person, to help you find your own answers to a problem or issue.

Pain
Pain is an unpleasant physical or emotional feeling that your body produces as a warning sign that it has been damaged.

6 August 2007

⇨ The above information is reprinted with kind permission from NHS Direct. For more information on this and other health-related issues, visit www.nhsdirect.nhs.uk

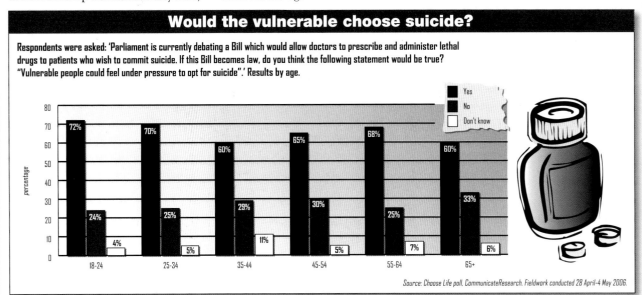

Would the vulnerable choose suicide?

Respondents were asked: 'Parliament is currently debating a Bill which would allow doctors to prescribe and administer lethal drugs to patients who wish to commit suicide. If this Bill becomes law, do you think the following statement would be true? "Vulnerable people could feel under pressure to opt for suicide".' Results by age.

Source: Choose Life poll, CommunicateResearch. Fieldwork conducted 28 April-4 May 2006.

Your body, your death, your choice?

Information from the Irish Council for Bioethics

Q1 What is euthanasia?

The word euthanasia stems from the Greek words 'eu thanatos' meaning 'good death' and refers to the action of a third party, usually a doctor to deliberately end the life of an individual. The individual must give consent for the procedure, which is known as voluntary euthanasia. Non-voluntary euthanasia occurs when the individual is unable to ask for the procedure e.g. if s/he is unconscious or otherwise unable to communicate and another person makes the decision on his/her behalf. In such cases the final decision might be based on the previously expressed wishes of the individual e.g. as stated in an advance healthcare directive (living will).

Assisted suicide refers to the practice of an individual taking his/her own life on the basis of information, guidance and/or medication provided by a third party. For example a doctor might prescribe a lethal dose of medication for an individual, who then administers the medication him/herself. (For a full list of definitions see table over page).

Q2 Is withdrawing and/or withholding treatment the same as euthanasia?

In certain circumstances treatments may be withheld or withdrawn from a patient because their provision would no longer be deemed to be in the best interest of the patient. For instance, if a treatment is considered futile, i.e. it offers a low probability of success or its provision would be overly burdensome on a patient, then it may be withheld. Also if a treatment is initiated but becomes a burden on the individual and no longer offers any therapeutic benefit then it may be withdrawn.

Q3 What is the principle of double effect?

When euthanising a patient, the doctor intends to cause the death of the individual. It is this intention that distinguishes euthanasia from other medical practices, which might also result in an individual's death. For example, if a patient is in severe pain, a doctor may prescribe pain medication, the intention of which is to ease the patient's suffering. However, in some cases the dose of pain medication required to relieve the pain may also be sufficient to end that patient's life. This is known as the doctrine of double effect since the treatment provided to ease pain has the additional effect of ending the patient's life.

Q4 Does an individual have the right to choose how and when to die?

It is generally accepted that as an expression of autonomy, i.e. one's right to make independent choices without any external influences, a competent adult can refuse medical treatment, even in situations where this could result in his/her death. However, when it comes to actively ending a life via euthanasia there is widespread debate regarding the rights of an individual to make that choice. Proponents argue that euthanasia allows terminally ill people to die with dignity and without pain and state that society should permit people to opt for euthanasia if they so wish. Proponents also state that individuals should be free to dictate the time and place of their own death. Finally, proponents argue that forcing people to live against their wishes violates personal freedoms and human rights and that it is immoral to compel people to continue to live with unbearable pain and suffering. Opponents of euthanasia, on religious grounds, argue that life is a gift from God and that only God has the power to take it away. Others contend that individuals don't get to decide when and how they are born, therefore, they should not be allowed to decide how and when they die. They also raise concerns that allowing euthanasia could lead to an abuse of power where people might be euthanised when they don't actually wish to die.

Q5 Does personal autonomy have limitations?

Few decisions are as important as those related to end-of-life healthcare. While an individual might want to express his/her autonomy by deciding to end his/her life, that decision will, in all likelihood, be influenced by the views of third parties, i.e. the individual's doctor, family or friends. Proponents of euthanasia argue that the decision to end a life of pain and suffering is an expression of one's right to personal autonomy, which should be respected by one's family, healthcare providers and society at large. However, opponents argue that because we live in an interdependent society, where one's decisions will impact on others physically, emotionally and financially, limits should be placed on personal autonomy in relation to end-of-life healthcare choices.

Opponents have raised concerns about the implications legalising euthanasia would have for society. They state that governments have a duty to protect society as a whole, as opposed to individual citizens, and that allowing euthanasia could harm society. Therefore, they argue that governments should balance an individual's right to die against potential negative consequences for the wider community. On the other hand, proponents argue that society is made up of individual citizens, whose rights should be protected, and that if euthanasia is properly regulated then the rights of society would not be harmed.

Q6 Does euthanasia devalue life?

It has been argued that permitting euthanasia could diminish respect for life. Concerns have been raised that allowing euthanasia for terminally ill individuals who request it, could result in a situation where all terminally ill individuals would feel pressurised into availing of euthanasia. There are fears that such individuals might begin to view themselves as a burden on their family, friends and society or as a strain on limited healthcare resources. Opponents of euthanasia also contend that permitting individuals to end their lives may lead to a situation where certain groups within society e.g. the terminally ill, severely disabled individuals or the elderly would be euthanised as a rule.

However, proponents of euthanasia argue that legalising the practice would not devalue life or result in pressure being put on individuals to end their lives but would allow those with no hope of recovery to die with dignity and without unnecessary suffering. They state that it would be imprudent not to implement legislation because this would drive euthanasia underground where it would be unregulated. They also raise concerns that the current legal vacuum has led to many Irish people travelling abroad (while they are still physically able to) to avail of euthanasia/assisted suicide before they feel they are ready to die.

Opponents state that suffering assists in forming personal identity and ,therefore, argue against euthanasia. However, proponents argue that there is no value in suffering and state that individuals who have no hope of recovery should not be obliged to suffer unduly.

Q7 Would legalising euthanasia undermine the level of healthcare provided?

There are fears that allowing euthanasia would encourage the practice to become the norm, as it might be easier and cheaper to provide than other forms of end-of-life healthcare.

Palliative care attempts to improve the quality of life for patients facing a life-threatening or life-limiting illness through the prevention and relief of pain and other symptoms, including physical, psychological, social and spiritual problems. However, it has been estimated that in a minority of cases (approximately 5%) an individual's pain cannot be eased with palliative drug treatment and concerns have been raised regarding the

profound spiritual and psychological suffering experienced by individuals faced with their imminent death.

Opponents of euthanasia argue that more resources should be put into palliative care, which allows people to die with dignity and which offers support and comfort to family and friends. Proponents argue, however, that individuals might prefer to die on their own terms and at a time of their choosing and suggest that euthanasia should be offered as a viable alternative for those individuals who are not satisfied with palliative care.

Q8 Is euthanasia only an issue for the terminally ill?

While euthanasia is often associated with terminally ill patients, there have been suggestions that voluntary euthanasia might also be relevant to very elderly individuals, individuals with chronic or degenerative illness, individuals with mental health problems and society as a whole. One area of healthcare where euthanasia has been widely debated of late is in the care of severely premature babies.

In effect, the same treatment and care decisions apply for extremely premature babies (those born after only 22-25 weeks of pregnancy) as with end-of-life care decisions for adults, i.e. should treatment be administered or should the baby be allowed to die. For extremely premature babies, the chances of survival can be very low, and those babies who do survive can show increased incidence of serious and long-lasting health problems. Some would argue that, because of potential future health risks, extremely premature babies should not be made to suffer and argue that under such circumstances euthanasia for babies would be acceptable. On the other hand, opponents state that euthanasia

should never be considered in such cases because they believe that all possible treatment should be provided to give severely premature babies every opportunity to survive and potentially live a normal life.

Q9 Where is euthanasia and/or assisted suicide legal?

There are a number of different jurisdictions, which allow euthanasia and/or assisted suicide to varying degrees. In Europe, euthanasia is only legal in the Netherlands and Belgium, provided certain conditions are met. For example, the patient's request must be voluntary and well-considered; the patient must be experiencing unbearable physical or mental suffering, with no prospect of relief; the patient must be informed about their situation and prospects; at least one other, independent, doctor must be consulted. In Belgium euthanasia is only allowed if the patient is an adult. However, in the Netherlands euthanasia is allowed for children aged between 12 and 16 years of age, with the consent of their parents/guardians and for individuals aged 16 years and over. Assisted suicide is legal in the Netherlands, Switzerland and the state of Oregon in the US. As with euthanasia certain criteria need to be met before an individual's request for assisted suicide is followed, e.g. the patient must be considered competent and aware of their situation. In Oregon the individual requesting assisted suicide must be terminally ill, but in the Netherlands and Switzerland an individual need not have a terminal condition in order to request it.

⇨ Information from the Irish Council for Bioethics. Visit www.bioethics.ie for more information.

© Irish Council for Bioethics

Types of euthanasia

Terminology	Definition
Voluntary euthanasia	The action of a third party, which deliberately ends the life of an individual, with that individual's consent.
Non-voluntary euthanasia	Where the individual is unable to ask for euthanasia and another person makes the decision on his/her behalf, usually based on previously expressed wishes.
Assisted suicide	Where an individual takes his/her own life based on information, guidance and/or medication provided by a third party.
Physician assisted suicide	Where a doctor provides the information, guidance and/or medication with which an individual can take his/her own life.

Source: 'Euthanasia – Your Body, Your Death, Your Choice?', The Irish Council for Bioethics.

Euthanasia and assisted suicide

Q and A from Care NOT Killing

What are euthanasia and assisted suicide?

Euthanasia can be defined as 'the intentional killing by act or omission of a person whose life is felt not to be worth living'. Euthanasia can be:

1   Voluntary – where a competent patient requests it.
2   Involuntary – where a competent patient is not consulted.
3   Non-voluntary – where the patient is not competent to make the request.

Euthanasia is usually carried out by a doctor administering lethal drugs, for example, by injection. Physician-assisted suicide (PAS) is where a doctor prescribes lethal drugs for the patient to take himself. Both euthanasia and assisted suicide are currently illegal in Britain.

What are the main arguments against legalising euthanasia?

The main reasons given for not legalising euthanasia are that it is:

1   Unnecessary – because alternative treatments exist.
2   Dangerous – putting vulnerable people at risk.
3   Wrong – contrary to all historical codes of ethics.

Isn't it cruel to deprive suffering people of an end to their pain?

Requests for euthanasia and assisted suicide are extremely rare when patients' needs, including physical, social, psychological and spiritual needs, are properly met. Therefore we believe that our key priority should be to build on the excellent tradition of palliative care that we have in this country and make palliative care more readily accessible to all who need it. We believe we need to get rid of the postcode lottery of palliative care in this country and promote care rather than killing. The vast majority of people dying in the UK, even from diseases like motor neurone

disease (from which 1,000 people die every year in the UK, in the main comfortably with good palliative care), do not want euthanasia or assisted suicide. The very small numbers of high profile cases of assisted suicide, which are regularly and repeatedly highlighted in the media, are well-publicised exceptions to the rule. The real question is therefore whether we should change the law for a very small number of people who are strongly determined to end their lives. We believe that to do so would place the lives of a much larger number of vulnerable people in danger and mean that pressure, whether real or imagined, is felt by sick, disabled and elderly people to request early death.

Aren't doctors already prescribing medicine knowing that it will result in the death of the patient (e.g. cancer patients)? – what is the difference between this and euthanasia/PAS?

Very rarely when strong narcotics like morphine are given to patients who are terminally ill they may have the secondary effect of shortening life – although with good palliative care this occurs in less than one case in a thousand. This is known as the principle of 'double effect' – when an action has two effects – one good and one bad. The good effect of relieving the pain is intended. The bad effect of shortening life is foreseen but not intended. If a patient dies as a result of double effect that is both ethical and legal. Having said that, if pain is being appropriately treated with narcotics double effect seldom if ever occurs because the toxic dose (which kills the patient) is virtually always higher than the therapeutic dose (which relieves pain). It is virtually always possible therefore for a skilled palliative care physician to kill the pain without killing the patient. On very rare occasions very close to death it may be necessary to sedate a patient to relieve the pain adequately, but even here it is almost invariably the disease process which kills rather than the treatment.

What is the difference between withholding a treatment because it is futile and intentionally causing a death through act or omission? Are these not merely semantic differences?

Some people distinguish 'active' euthanasia – administering a lethal injection – from 'passive' euthanasia – withholding or withdrawing treatment. This distinction is un-helpful and confusing because there are a significant number of cases where withholding or withdrawing treatment can be good medical practice. The distinction between euthanasia and good medical practice hinges

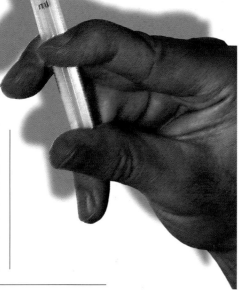

on the intention with which a treatment is given or withheld. In euthanasia the intention is to kill; in good medical practice it is to maximise the quality of life experienced by the patient.

Requests for euthanasia and assisted suicide are extremely rare when patients' needs, including physical, social, psychological and spiritual needs, are properly met

---

Some treatments are medically useless in that the suffering that they cause outweighs any benefit they bring. Stopping or not starting a medically useless treatment is not euthanasia. But there is a world of difference between saying that a treatment is useless (and therefore not worth giving) and that a patient is useless (and therefore not worth treating). In the same way if a competent patient refuses life-saving medical treatment and dies as a result, that is not euthanasia. Doctors cannot force patients to have treatment against their wills. If a patient who is capable of deciding refuses a life-saving treatment – then the doctor is not performing euthanasia by not forcing it upon them against their will.

If the government won't fund palliative care properly, why should people not choose to end their pain through euthanasia or assisted suicide?

The proper response of a responsible government is to ensure that there is adequate funding to provide palliative care for all who need it. Good palliative care may depend on skilled personnel but it is neither technologically difficult nor expensive to provide. But this question about funding highlights an important danger. If the law is ever changed to allow so-called 'assisted dying' it is inevitable that economic pressure will be brought to bear on people, openly

or more likely very subtly, to request early death in order to save money for the use of relatives, society or a health service short of the resources it needs. Killing is very cost effective – it does not cost much for an ampoule of barbiturate. That is why we need to promote care, not killing, and hold onto laws which protect vulnerable people.

What are the main arguments for euthanasia?

There are three main arguments for euthanasia.

➪ We want it – the autonomy argument.
➪ We need it – the compassion argument.
➪ We can control it – the public policy argument.

The debate in the 1990s centred on the compassion argument, but because of cultural changes and palliative care's success, has moved to arguments based on autonomy.

What is autonomy?

Autonomy means 'self-determination' and the language heard now in the euthanasia debate is often that of choice, control, freedoms and rights. The euthanasia lobby's thrust, as evidenced in Lord Joffe's Bill, has moved from euthanasia as a needed response to symptoms to euthanasia as an autonomous choice by those with, for example, degenerative neurological disease.

Shouldn't euthanasia and assisted suicide be a matter of free choice?

Autonomy is important but we have laws because autonomy is not absolute. We all value living in a free society but also recognise that we are not free to do things which threaten the reasonable freedoms of others. Legalising euthanasia would actually undermine people's autonomy for four reasons.

1 Most people who ask for euthanasia do not actually want it.
2 Vulnerable people will feel pressure to request euthanasia.
3 Euthanasia cannot be controlled.
4 Euthanasia would change the nature of medicine.

On what basis can you say that most people who ask for euthanasia do not actually want it?

Those caring for the dying know that the (relatively few) who currently ask for euthanasia usually have another question behind their question. This may be physical – a distressing symptom needs palliation; psychosocial – they may want an honest discussion with their family; emotional – they may be depressed; or spiritual – wanting answers to 'Why me?' and 'Why now?' Depression is particularly common in terminally ill patients and leads to suicidal thoughts; and yet in most cases it can be effectively treated. Requests for euthanasia are extremely rare when patients are properly cared for and physical, psychosocial, emotional and spiritual needs are properly met. Our key priority must therefore be to make the highest quality palliative care more widely available. This is true compassion.

Why would vulnerable people feel pressure to request euthanasia?

In 1994 a House of Lords Select Committee reported on euthanasia, and unanimously recommended no change in the law. Its Chairman, neurologist Lord Walton of Detchant, later described in Parliament their concerns about such legislation: 'We concluded that it was virtually impossible to ensure that all acts of euthanasia were truly voluntary and that any liberalisation of the law in the United Kingdom could not be abused. We were also concerned that vulnerable people – the elderly, lonely, sick or distressed – would feel pressure, whether real or imagined, to request early death.' People who are dying often feel a burden on relatives, carers and a society short of resources. A law allowing euthanasia would place them under huge pressure.

On what basis can you say that euthanasia cannot be controlled?

The progression from voluntary to non-voluntary or involuntary euthanasia is well documented in the Netherlands. The *Remmelink Report* analysed all 129,000 deaths in the Netherlands in 1990. 3% were by euthanasia. Of that 3%, one in three, 1% of all deaths in the Netherlands in 1990, were euthanasia 'without explicit request'. In a mix of non-voluntary and involuntary euthanasia, Dutch doctors in 1990 killed more than 1,000 patients without their request. This level of euthanasia has continued and now about half of all Dutch euthanasia deaths are not even reported. Furthermore in 2005 Dutch doctors instituted the Groningen protocol enabling the killing of severely disabled children. Legalising euthanasia here would give doctors power they should not be entitled to have and would mean that economic and convenience factors would inevitably start to influence decision-making. Doctors could become the most dangerous people in the state.

How would euthanasia change the shape of medicine?

Legalising PAS and euthanasia would split the medical profession. 75% of doctors in a major poll (*Hospital Doctor*, 15 May 2003) have already indicated that they will not participate in euthanasia if it is legalised, and a change in the law, as in the case of abortion, will lead to doctors who conscientiously object being excluded from specialities where euthanasia becomes part of the 'full range of services'. Euthanasia legislation would have a devastating effect throughout the National Health Service on already critical levels of staffing, where we are reliant especially on many overseas nurses from Muslim, Christian and other faith backgrounds who are strongly opposed to the practice.

Shouldn't PAS be allowed just for the very difficult cases?

The law is a blunt instrument, and there will always be individual cases, usually those that have not been managed well, which raise questions about PAS. But hard cases make bad laws. Any law allowing PAS would threaten the trust necessary for the doctor–patient relationship to function, place pressure on patients to request early death, and introduce a slippery slope to voluntary and involuntary euthanasia. Such legislation would also be impossible to police, might well undermine the development of palliative-care services, and could lead to patients being incited to request suicide for economic reasons by family, carers, or society at large.

Why do some people argue that euthanasia is morally wrong?

Many people are convinced by the arguments already given above but go further to argue that euthanasia is fundamentally wrong. Euthanasia is certainly against the Hippocratic Oath ('I will give no deadly medicine to anyone if asked') and in like manner the World Medical Association reaffirmed in 2005 that 'physician assisted suicide, like euthanasia is unethical and must be condemned by the medical profession'. In addition euthanasia runs contrary to the Judeo-Christian ethic on which our laws are based. The belief that euthanasia is fundamentally wrong is also present in Judaism, Islam, Sikhism, Buddhism and Hinduism. Nine UK faith leaders representing the six major world faiths recently wrote to every member of both Houses of Parliament opposing any change in the law.

Isn't physician-assisted suicide (PAS) a safer option than euthanasia?

Because of the difficulties in getting voluntary euthanasia (VE) accepted the pro-euthanasia lobby have directed their attention to the seemingly softer target of physician-assisted suicide (PAS). It was calculated by a recent House of Lords Select Committee that a Netherlands-type law (VE and PAS) would lead to 13,000 new deaths per annum in Britain, whereas an Oregon-type law (PAS only) would lead to 650 deaths per annum.

But in fact VE and PAS are ethically equivalent because in both cases the intention of the doctor is to end the life of the patient. There is little practical difference between placing lethal medication in a patient's hand and placing it in a patient's mouth! PAS is simply 'euthanasia one step back'.

Legalising PAS would also bring in euthanasia because of:

⇨ **Incapacity.** Some patients would be physically incapable of ending their own lives (e.g. through paralysis) so VE back-up would be required.

⇨ **Failure rates.** Even with a prescription, PAS has a failure rate. Some patients vomit, while others fail to die despite large doses of drugs. In these situations, a doctor will always be required for the coup de grâce.

⇨ **Incremental extension.** Once doctors begin practising PAS there will be those who will 'push the limits' and euthanasia will inevitably follow. When the patient – the 'key witness' – is dead, who is to say whether it was suicide or euthanasia?

How does the medical profession view euthanasia?

Doctors have historically always been opposed to both euthanasia and assisted suicide. The Hippocratic Oath forbids both as do more recent codes of ethics such as the Declaration of Geneva and the International Code of Medical Ethics. The majority of doctors in the UK remain opposed to assisted dying and medical opposition has actually intensified in recent years. The largest most recent surveys show only 22-38% of doctors in favour of a change in the law. This was made very clear to the recent House of Lords Select Committee examining Lord Joffe's Assisted Dying for the Terminally Ill Bill. The opposition to euthanasia is strongest amongst doctors who work most closely with dying patients and are most familiar with treatments available. One of our steering group members is the Association for Palliative Medicine of Great Britain & Ireland, which represents over 800 UK specialists in palliative care. Well over 90% of its members are strongly opposed to euthanasia. The Royal College of General Practitioners (RCGP), the Royal College of Anaesthetists, the Royal College of Surgeons of Edinburgh, the Royal College of Nursing and the British Geriatric Society also remain strongly opposed to euthanasia. Other colleges such as the Royal College of Psychiatrists and the Royal College of Physicians are currently reconsidering their positions. Whilst some Royal Colleges have declined to take a position, largely because they do not deal directly with dying patients, no Royal College is in favour of a change in the law. The BMA itself does not favour a change in the law and the recent and much-publicised vote at the BMA annual conference to adopt a position of neutrality towards any future bill was unrepresentative of the Association's 134,000 members. It was carried by a very narrow majority (93 votes to 82) at a barely quorate meeting on the last day of the conference when over half of the delegates had either left or were otherwise engaged.

Isn't the public generally in favour of euthanasia?

There has been much recent publicity to the effect that most people are in favour of a change in the law. But most polls of this nature are based on answers to Yes/No or Either/Or questions without any explanatory context and without other options – e.g. good quality palliative care – being offered. In other words the answer you get depends very much on how you ask the question. If you ask people if they would like help to die comfortably, most will say yes. If you ask them if they would like to receive a lethal injection most will say no. Most people have little understanding of the complexities and dangers in changing the law in this way and opinion research consists therefore to a large extent of knee-jerk answers to emotive – and often leading – questions. In addition those most in favour of euthanasia tend to be the 'worried well'. Requests for euthanasia from people who are dying or who are disabled are very rare indeed, provided they are being properly cared for.

30 January 2006

⇨ The above information is reprinted with kind permission from Care NOT Killing. Visit www.carenotkilling.org.uk for more information.

© Care NOT Killing

We must help people die with dignity

By Sarah Wootton

The case of Robert Cook who killed his terminally ill wife Vanessa made national headlines. He was given a 12-month jail sentence suspended for two years after he admitted manslaughter on the grounds of diminished responsibility and aiding and abetting his 55-year-old wife's suicide.

Sarah Wootton, chief executive of Dignity in Dying, says the law must be changed to allow terminally ill people to die when they choose.

Friday marked the end of what was a sad, drawn-out and unnecessary process for Robert Cook.

The 60-year-old lost his wife in October 2006 to multiple sclerosis (MS).

His wife Vanessa had MS diagnosed in 2003 and had reached the point where she could not take any more suffering.

Mrs Cook, 55, wanted to die and had tried to commit suicide several times. Upon her final attempt she asked her husband to ensure that she was successful.

Robert was present when his wife took an overdose and he put a plastic bag over her head to ensure she did not wake up.

Mr Cook, of Camber Close, Crawley, was placed in a situation that most of us will never have to endure.

Yet, the unfortunate few like Mr Cook will face the terrible responsibility of having to decide between their conscience and the law when a loved one asks for help to die.

Mr Cook's family described him as a 'loving and devoted husband' and said that he and his wife were 'like peas in a pod'. Vanessa's brother and sister both described Mr Cook's actions as 'brave and unselfish'.

This was reflected in the judge's decision to spare Mr Cook jail on the grounds of diminished responsibility.

Both the jury and the judge recognised that before them stood a brave and innocent man who had acted out of nothing but love and devotion for his wife up until her dying moment. Yet Mr Cook was vilified and treated like a criminal.

It is unacceptable that at a time when he should have been treated with compassion and allowed to grieve for his wife in peace, he was arrested, charged with murder and then forced to wait more than 18 months to know whether or not he would be sent to prison.

The current law fails terminally ill people and their loved ones.

Assisted suicide is happening every day, behind closed doors, as it becomes apparent to terminally ill people there is no medical or legal help available to them if they wish to die.

The current law fails terminally ill people and their loved ones

The law must change to allow terminally ill, mentally competent adults the right to ask a doctor for help to die at a time and place of their choosing.

More than 80 per cent of the British public are compassionate enough to recognise that when suffering and indignity become too

much to bear, a person should have the right to choose.

Medically assisted dying is already available in countries across the world. Oregon introduced this right in 1997 and was later found to be the second best state in which to die in the US.

Evidence shows the assisted dying legislation has prevented many violent suicides. It has given people the reassurance that, if their condition ever becomes too much to bear, they have the option of dying peacefully, painlessly and surrounded by loved ones.

Evidence from Oregon also shows only one in 200 who request information about medically assisted dying actually go through with it.

For many, it is the peace of mind the option is there that is so valuable.

Unfortunately, our law denies people like Vanessa and Mr Cook this reassurance.

Assisting the suicide of another without proper medical assistance is extremely dangerous and traumatic.

It is a crime punishable by up to 14 years in prison.

Yet many people will see no alternative.

Until the law is changed, we will continue to see cases where people have been forced to take matters into their own hands.

Palliative care is an equally important part of end-of-life care.

It should also be a basic right of any terminally ill person to receive adequate support and care in the final stages of their illness.

It is also important to recognise that palliative care, regardless of its standard, is not always enough for some people to alleviate the constant suffering and indignity they endure at the hands of these terrible diseases.

Furthermore, evidence from Oregon shows that assisted dying can form part of a compassionate palliative care system that is flexible and recognises that the needs and wishes of each individual are unique.

It is time the vocal minority opposing assisted dying recognised that their views are resulting in the extended suffering of many terminally ill people, who want nothing more than to die with dignity.

Nobody has the right to deny a person this choice.

It is time the law was changed to allow medically assisted dying for adults who are suffering unbearably.

It is time we allowed people real choices at the end of their lives.

It is common sense that the law needs to be changed if cases like Robert Cook's are to be avoided.

For more information about Dignity in Dying, telephone 0870 7777868 or visit www.dignity indying. org.uk.

5 February 2008

⇨ The above information is reprinted with kind permission from Brighton-based newspaper *The Argus*. Visit www.theargus.co.uk for more information.

© *The Argus*

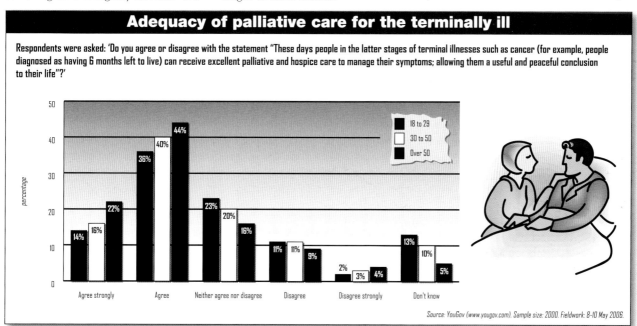

Adequacy of palliative care for the terminally ill

Respondents were asked: 'Do you agree or disagree with the statement "These days people in the latter stages of terminal illnesses such as cancer (for example, people diagnosed as having 6 months left to live) can receive excellent palliative and hospice care to manage their symptoms; allowing them a useful and peaceful conclusion to their life"?'

Legend: 18 to 29, 30 to 50, Over 50

	Agree strongly	Agree	Neither agree nor disagree	Disagree	Disagree strongly	Don't know
18 to 29	14%	36%	23%	11%	2%	13%
30 to 50	16%	40%	20%	11%	3%	10%
Over 50	22%	44%	16%	9%	4%	5%

Source: YouGov (www.yougov.com). Sample size: 2000. Fieldwork: 8-10 May 2006.

Answering the euthanasia critics

Brief answers to five objections

OBJECTION 1 – We cannot always be sure that the patient wants to die

Answer: There are no absolute certainties in medical practice but this does not eliminate the need, at times, for doctors to make life-and-death decisions. Faced with a request for euthanasia, the doctor would follow prescribed guidelines which would include being satisfied that the strength and persistence of the request left no reasonable doubt as to the patient's firm and rational intention.

OBJECTION 2 – We cannot always be sure that there is no possibility of cure or return to an acceptable quality of life

Answer: Cures take years to discover, test and become generally available. The doctor would discuss the prognosis so that the patient could make an informed decision as to whether a cure or remission was worth waiting for.

OBJECTION 3 – Palliative care is now so effective that no one need ever ask for euthanasia

Answer: There are acknowledged limits to palliative care. There are still cases in which pain cannot be satisfactorily controlled, but of greater concern is the loss of faculties and descent into total dependence on others over a lengthy period as a miserable prelude to death. The June 2002 Morgan Poll revealed that only 23% of those polled considered that palliative care was sufficient.

> **There are no absolute certainties in medical practice but this does not eliminate the need, at times, for doctors to make life-and-death decisions**

OBJECTION 4 – Efforts to find cures and to improve palliative care will be discouraged

Answer: The will to live is so strong that no one wishes to die while their life can still have reasonable quality. There will always be pressure to find cures and improve treatment. Euthanasia would only be an option for those whom current medical skills could not help. The incentive to perfect those skills would remain.

OBJECTION 5 – It is always wrong to shorten life deliberately

Answer: Those who have this conviction would be free to abstain, either as doctor or patient, but should not deny the option to those who do not share their belief. Most people hold that life should not be taken unlawfully: they accept that there are circumstances in which the taking of life at the request of the patient may be justified and that the law should provide for these.

⇨ The above information is reprinted with kind permission from the South Australian Voluntary Euthanasia Society. Visit www.saves.asn.au for more information.

© Australian Voluntary Euthanasia Society

A dubious distinction

People are allowed to refuse medical treatment, yet doctors still cannot assist a patient's death

On December 21 an Italian doctor, Mario Riccio, disconnected a respirator that was keeping Piergiorgio Welby alive. Welby, who suffered from muscular dystrophy and was paralysed, had battled unsuccessfully in the Italian courts for the right to die. He said, 'Thank you', three times to his wife, his friends and his doctor. Forty-five minutes later, he was dead.

His request to die led to heated

By Peter Singer

debate in Italy, and it is unclear whether Riccio will be charged with any offence. At least one Italian politician has called for his arrest on a charge of murder.

Welby's death raises two questions – whether a person has a right to refuse life-sustaining medical treatment; and whether voluntary euthanasia is ethically defensible.

A patient's informed consent should be a prerequisite for all medical treatment, as long as the patient is a competent adult in a position to make a decision. Forcing medical treatment on such a patient who does not want it is tantamount to assault. We may think that the patient is making the wrong decision, but we should respect his or her right to make it. That right is recognised in most countries, but not, apparently, in Italy.

Even the Roman Catholic Church has long held that there is no obligation to use 'extraordinary' or 'disproportionate' means to prolong life – a view reiterated in the Declaration on Euthanasia issued by the Sacred Congregation for the Doctrine of the Faith and approved by Pope John Paul II in 1980. That document states that to refuse burdensome medical treatment 'is not the equivalent of suicide' but 'should be considered an acceptance of the human condition, or a wish to avoid the application of a medical procedure disproportionate to the results that can be expected, or a desire not to impose excessive expense on the family or the community'.

A patient's informed consent should be a prerequisite for all medical treatment, as long as the patient is a competent adult in a position to make a decision

---

On that basis, Riccio was doing what anyone should have been prepared to do for Welby, who was unable to implement his refusal of burdensome medical treatment. So the case falls on the right side of the line drawn by Catholic doctrine, but does church doctrine draw the line in a sensible place? If an incurably ill patient can refuse burdensome treatment, knowing that this refusal will mean his or her death, why should an incurably ill patient who is not being kept alive by any medical treatment, but finds that the illness itself makes life burdensome, be unable to seek assistance in escaping that burden?

Defenders of Catholic teaching would answer that the latter patient intends to end his or her life, whereas the former patient merely intends to avoid the additional burden that treatment brings. Death is a foreseeable consequence of avoiding that burden, but it is a byproduct, not directly intended. If the patient could avoid the burden and yet continue to live, that would be his choice. Welby should not have been helped to die, they might argue, because he expressly said that he wanted to die, not that he wanted to avoid burdensome treatment.

This distinction is dubious. Both patients knowingly choose a course of action that will lead to death, rather than to a longer but burdensome life. By focusing on the intention to refuse burdensome treatment, rather than the broader implications of the choice, the church avoids the inhumane implication that patients must accept life-prolonging treatment, no matter how painful or costly it may be. But it does so at the cost of rendering incoherent its own vigorous opposition to assisted suicide and voluntary euthanasia.

Many countries recognise a legal right to refuse medical treatment. But only in the Netherlands, Belgium, Switzerland and the US state of Oregon are doctors allowed to assist a patient in ending his or her life by means other than withdrawing life-sustaining treatment.

The Netherlands, in particular, has been subjected to a relentless campaign of vilification. Critics allege that the legalisation of voluntary euthanasia has led to a breakdown of trust in the medical profession and all sorts of other dire consequences. But if these allegations are true, no one has told the Dutch. Despite a change of government in the Netherlands since voluntary euthanasia was legalised, no effort has been made to repeal the measure. There is simply no public support for such a move.

The Dutch know how voluntary euthanasia is practised in their country, they know that legal euthanasia has improved, rather than harmed, their medical care, and they want the possibility of assistance in dying. Isn't that a choice that everyone should have?

⇨ Peter Singer is professor of bioethics at Princeton University; his books include *Practical Ethics* and *Rethinking Life and Death*. www.project-syndicate.org

17 January 2007

© *Guardian Newspapers Limited 2007*

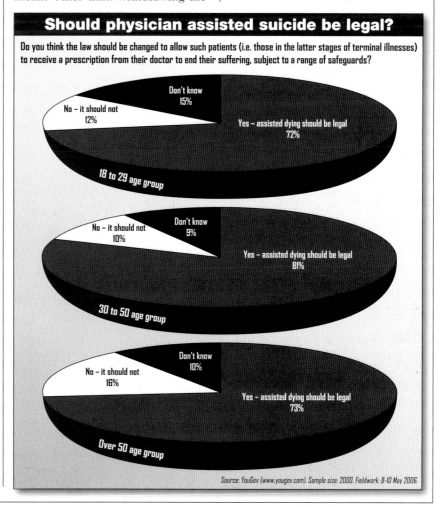

Should physician assisted suicide be legal?

Do you think the law should be changed to allow such patients (i.e. those in the latter stages of terminal illnesses) to receive a prescription from their doctor to end their suffering, subject to a range of safeguards?

18 to 29 age group
- Don't know 15%
- No – it should not 12%
- Yes – assisted dying should be legal 72%

30 to 50 age group
- No – it should not 10%
- Don't know 9%
- Yes – assisted dying should be legal 81%

Over 50 age group
- No – it should not 16%
- Don't know 10%
- Yes – assisted dying should be legal 73%

Source: YouGov (www.yougov.com). Sample size: 2000. Fieldwork: 8-10 May 2006.

Public opinion on medically assisted dying

New survey shows overwhelming public support for a law allowing medically assisted dying for the terminally ill

Anew YouGov survey, released today, has shown that the majority of adults are in favour of a law allowing medically assisted dying.

76% of respondents either agreed or strongly agreed that terminally ill people should be allowed medical assistance to die. 56% agreed or strongly agreed that those with a non-terminal but incurable illness should also be allowed medical help to die upon request.

76% of respondents either agreed or strongly agreed that terminally ill people should be allowed medical assistance to die

The results are consistent with those of previous surveys, which have indicated overwhelming public support of medically assisted dying for the terminally ill.

Sarah Wootton, Chief Executive of Dignity in Dying, which campaigns

Dignity
in dying
your life, your choice

for the legalisation of medically assisted dying for the terminally ill, said:

'This latest survey once again shows that the majority of the public recognise the right to die as a fundamental choice at the end of life. It is common sense that people who are terminally ill, mentally competent and suffering unbearably should be allowed the option of medically assisted dying.'

The results of the YouGov survey coincide with publication of a new book examining the ethical, medical and philosophical arguments on either side of the assisted dying debate. The book, written by Baroness Mary Warnock and Dr. Elisabeth Macdonald, was motivated by the growing movement

in many countries to legalise some form of assisted dying.

Wootton continued:

'There are instances where palliative care, regardless of high standards, is not enough to alleviate the constant suffering and loss of dignity that some terminally ill people endure in the final stages of their illnesses.

'This latest survey once again shows that the majority of the public recognise the right to die as a fundamental choice at the end of life'

'The law must change to allow people this choice.'
10 March 2008

⇨ The above information is reprinted with kind permission from Dignity in Dying. Please visit their website at www.dignityindying.org. uk for more information on this and other related issues.
© Dignity in Dying

What do the public think?

A poll published today allegedly shows that three quarters of Brits think euthanasia should be legalised. The poll, conducted by YouGov, also found that 56% of people felt that those with non-terminal but incurable illness should also be allowed medical assistance to die upon request

Time for change?

Pro-euthanasia groups have welcomed the poll as showing public support for their cause - Sarah Wootton of Dignity In Dying said: 'The law must change to allow people this choice'.

However, contrary to what has been stated in recent news reports, it is not true that Britain's law is out of step with the rest of Europe, nor is it true that 'many countries have legalised some form of assisted dying'.

Majority support for a change in the law is quite common in polls about emotive issues where people are invited to air their views on matters where they often don't have access to the facts

---

It is true that European countries deal with euthanasia and assisted suicide in various different way under their penal codes and impose different penalties for breaking their laws. However, only in Belgium, the Netherlands and Luxembourg is euthanasia legal. Furthermore, only a handful of countries allow physician assisted suicide. So, it is British law that reflects the European 'norm'.

Public opinion

Public opinion polls often do show majority support for a change in the law. But this phenomenon is quite common in polls about emotive issues – e.g. capital punishment, immigration – where people are invited to air their views on matters where they often don't have access to the facts...

⇨ Advances in palliative care, of which there is often insufficient

awareness, have largely removed requests for euthanasia.

⇨ There are real dangers in legalising an option which, despite appearing desirable to a few determined people, could create subtle pressures on dying people at a vulnerable time of their lives.

⇨ Terminally ill people are highly dependent on the advice they receive from their physicians. Physicians are not uniformly competent or altruistic, and some dying people could end up taking irrevocable decisions based of inadequate advice.

⇨ Where euthanasia has been legalised, palliative care is not a recognised medical speciality as it is in Britain.

⇨ It's all very well to talk about 'safeguards', but the ones we have seen to date in recent 'assisted dying' bills have been paper-thin.

Questions & Answers

Also, it depends what question you ask as to what answer you get. In May 2006 a Communicate Research Poll reported on this site showed the following:

⇨ Opposition to the proposal that doctors should be allowed to 'prescribe and administer lethal drugs to patients who wish to commit suicide'. 65% of people agreed that if such a change went ahead, 'vulnerable people could feel under pressure to opt for suicide.

⇨ Concern that such a change in the law might put doctors under pressure. 72% of people agreed that 'doctors and other healthcare workers with ethical objections might feel under pressure to comply'.

⇨ Agreement that some patients would feel under pressure to opt for suicide. 75% of people agreed that 'people with treatable illness such as depression might opt prematurely for suicide'.

⇨ Agreement by 73% that it would 'make it more difficult to detect rogue doctors such as Dr Harold Shipman'.

Doctors themselves recognise these dangers, which is one reason why the great majority of them want nothing at all to do with 'assisted dying'.
11 March 2008

⇨ The above information is reprinted with kind permission from Care NOT Killing. Please visit their website at www.carenotkilling.org.uk for more information.

Euthanasia: 'we should not be made to suffer like this'

As Luxembourg joins Holland and Belgium in legalising euthanasia, Val McKay, terminally ill with multiple sclerosis, tells Jocasta Shakespeare why the law in Britain should change

Two scythe-wielding skeletons are stencilled on the mauve walls. She smiles: 'People think I'm morbid, but Death is welcome here; I'm not afraid. He hasn't been too helpful yet, though.'

It's not death Val is scared of but the process of dying. Her home in a quiet close of bungalows in Perth, Scotland, has become a prison. Four years ago, at the age of 46, she was diagnosed with multiple sclerosis, and since then her body has been shutting down, numbing from the feet up.

She is now unable to move her legs, right arm or lower body and is bed-ridden for 22 hours a day. She can get into a wheelchair only with the help of one of her carers, using a hoist.

Val's skin is smooth and line-free and her alert brown eyes express both humour and pain. Doctors say she may have just another six months to live. She thinks that is too long. 'This is torture. If I was Spooky my cat, I'd have been put down long ago.'

At the moment, Val can still use her hands to control the flat-screen television on the wall opposite her bed, to make phone calls and to smoke (a 20-a-day habit) but soon she will be deprived of even these simple pleasures. 'My left arm is going,' she says.

For now, she still has the power of speech and she intends to use it. 'I'll say what I want to say, I always have done. I want help to die. People like me should not be made to suffer like this. I'm angry that I'm not allowed help to die peacefully in my own home. I want to educate people about death. There should be a choice in how to die.'

Today, she wears rosy lipstick and her fingernails are manicured and polished with peach-coloured varnish.

'I'm dying but I'm still vain,' she jokes. She is also brave and defiant.

Most people who seek an assisted death dare not speak openly about it for fear of offending their families or of retribution from 'pro-Life' and religious groups. But Val is determined to challenge the law and the tiny 'moral' minority who support it. 'I want to speak out for those like me, or who come after me. The law is cruel and it is wrong.'

'The law is cruel and it is wrong'

She has considered suicide and once hoarded sleeping pills, but she realised she would be found by her carers and taken to hospital. 'I didn't really know how to do it and thought I might bodge the job and end up even worse off,' she says.

But she fears the 'horrific natural death' that lies in store for her. She is likely to lose the ability to communicate and the swallowing reflex; she will then have to be 'peg fed' by a tube through her stomach and, as her airways close down, she may choke to death. Her brain will be the last organ affected.

She shows me a photograph of herself, taken at her 40th birthday party – a slim, smiling woman wearing a white dress and hoop earrings, cutting a cake. 'We had two cakes, so many people came!' Her eyes light up with joy at the memory.

'I was normal then. It was a great night and I'm glad I did it. I miss those times.' Separated from her husband, she had a boyfriend, David, a busy social life and was working as an accountant in a retail firm. 'I loved

my job, I loved my friends and I was very fond of David, but I gave them all up. I just couldn't bear them to see me like this.'

Her son Robert, from a previous marriage, is 26 years old and her happiest memory is the day her grandson, Matthew, was born. 'I looked in the crib and it was an overwhelming feeling of love; words just can't describe how I felt.'

Matthew is now seven, and it is this relationship that she finds hardest to relinquish. From her bed, Val can watch him bouncing on the trampoline in the garden when he comes to see her. 'I love him so much; if it wasn't for him, I'd have refused all treatment a long time ago.'

Refusing treatment is one way a terminally ill person can assert their will to die, but it requires huge reserves of willpower. Many patients are isolated in hospital or at home, surrounded by family and a medical profession intent on keeping them alive.

Val says she met a wall of silence when she first started questioning her situation: 'It was so frustrating, I couldn't find anyone to talk to.'

So she began a desperate search for information about the choices available to a dying person, searching the internet when her carers were out shopping, and watching television until late at night, hoping to find information and support – anything that would protect her from being kept alive against her will.

When she finally contacted the campaign group Dignity In Dying, last year, the relief was immense. 'It was wonderful to talk to someone who understands how I feel.'

Then she saw a television documentary about Dr Anne Turner, from Bath, who was in the early stages of an incurable degenerative disease, supranuclear palsy. At 66, Dr Turner, a family planning expert, had seen her husband and brother suffer lingering deaths.

With another five years left to live, she was determined to die on her own terms. In January 2006, she travelled to the Dignitas Clinic in Zurich, accompanied by her two daughters and sons. Swiss law allows assisted suicide but the person must prove mental competence and be able to voluntarily grasp and swallow a lethal sodium barbitol solution.

Once doctors at the clinic had agreed Dr Turner fulfilled the criteria, she was given the drugs and, accompanied by a nurse and her children, went to a nearby apartment where she died. No action was taken against her family on their return to Britain and they have since campaigned for a change in the law to allow assisted death for the terminally ill in the UK.

'When I saw Anne Turner on TV, I was so jealous,' Val says. 'I wanted to go there but didn't know how to do it.' She decided that she would prefer to die with the help of strangers in a rented room in a foreign country than to remain at the mercy of British doctors.

She talked to her family – they were shocked but have come to understand her position. Late last year, Val contacted FATE (Friends At The End), which is based in Scotland and allowed by Scottish law to publish information about Dignitas.

At first, just the thought that this option might be open to her gave Val relief. There were still practical problems: she would need to find someone to book her flight, get her to the airport, travel to the clinic and then watch while she took the drugs that would hasten her end.

Christmas interrupted her planning and, after enjoying the festivities with Matthew and her family, she decided not to contact Dignitas. 'I started to worry: what would Matthew think? That his Nan had done something criminal, had committed suicide?'

Now, two months later, as her condition has worsened, Val's resolve has vanished. She has a lung infection

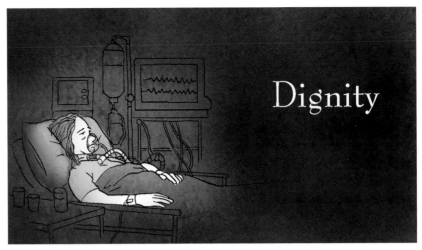

Dignity

and is taking strong antibiotics. 'I'm trapped, I've left it too late. I can stand a lot of pain, but it's getting worse. I've made up my mind I'm not going back to hospital.'

Doctors are not legally allowed to give adequate pain relief if this involves the 'double effect' of hastening death, and although she could still refuse food and hydration, she says her carers would not allow it.

When we last talked this week, her fierce will seemed broken and her voice was slurred and unutterably weary. 'I wish I'd gone to Switzerland. I can't go on, even for Matthew now, I can't go on,' she said.

Many will disagree strongly with Val's position, unable to contemplate allowing – let alone helping – a loved one to die under any circumstances. Instinctively, Val clings to life and especially the loving relationship she has with her grandson, but increasingly it is not enough.

She has reached the end of her own powers of physical and psychological endurance but has a long way to go until what she believes will be the bitterest of conclusions. The vacillation and regret she expresses as she struggles with the moral and practical issues of her desire for death illustrates her mental turmoil, but she dismisses suggestions that she is depressed or that better quality of care would improve her life and outlook.

What Val McKay wants is a dignified death over which she can exert some control, preferably assisted suicide, in her own home, surrounded by her family and her three carers, who have become her closest friends. 'I wasn't ready before Christmas and now I'm not well enough to go anywhere.

'Hindsight is a wonderful thing but I wish I'd gone to Zurich long ago. If I could just take something and it would all be over, it would be a huge relief.'

The British point of view

⇨ In May 2006, Lord Joffe's Assisted Dying for the Terminally Ill Bill, which would give doctors the right to prescribe drugs that a terminally ill patient in severe pain could use to end their own life, was defeated in the House of Lords.

Jeremy Purvis's subsequent attempt, in 2005, to introduce assisted death for the terminally ill and mentally competent was also defeated in the Scottish Parliament.

⇨ But 80 per cent of the British public support a change in the law to make medically assisted dying for terminally ill adults (who are suffering unbearably) a legal practice (British Social Attitudes survey, January 2007).

⇨ 81 per cent of Catholic respondents, 81 per cent of Protestants and 95 per cent of non-religious respondents support assisted dying legislation (NOP survey, 2004).

⇨ 80 per cent of disabled respondents supported assisted dying legislation (YouGov poll, 2004).

⇨ 78 per cent of people over 65 support a change in the law on assisted dying (NOP poll, 2004).

⇨ 80 British citizens have travelled to Dignitas in Switzerland to end their lives.

25 February 2008

Euthanasia: the legal issues

Information from the *Nursing Standard*

The current legal position

British law prohibits assisted dying. Practising active euthanasia would usually make an individual liable to be charged with murder (Wainwright 1999) and in English criminal law assisting someone to die carries a sentence of up to 14 years' imprisonment under the Suicide Act 1961.

In a number of high-profile legal cases, UK courts have consistently demonstrated that actively hastening the death of a patient via medical intervention is unlawful. For example, in *R v Cox* [1992], a patient, who was terminally ill and suffering from unrelievable pain, repeatedly requested that Dr Cox should end her life. When Dr Cox administered a lethal dose of potassium chloride with the intention that this would kill the patient, his actions were reported by a nurse and Dr Cox eventually received a one-year suspended prison sentence for attempted murder (Ferguson 1997).

The issues are sometimes muddled by the apparent inconsistency in the law's approach to medically assisted death

---

More recently, the case of Diane Pretty highlighted the legal prohibition of assisted suicide. Mrs Pretty was terminally ill and claimed that 'Right to life', article 2 of the Human Rights Act 1998, included the right to die, and to choose how and when to die. She unsuccessfully sought assurance from the court that her husband would not be prosecuted if he were to help her to die at a time of her own choosing (Dyer 2001). Although there was considerable support and sympathy for her plight, English law demonstrated its unwillingness to support assisted dying. The European Court of Human Rights ultimately rejected Mrs Pretty's case (Dyer 2002).

The issues are sometimes muddled by the apparent inconsistency in the law's approach to medically assisted death. For example, in 1999, a doctor, who openly advocated helping older patients to die with dignity, was acquitted on a charge of murder after he admitted giving a terminally ill patient a lethal dose of diamorphine with the intention of relieving pain rather than killing the patient (Wainwright 1999). For further discussion on the issue

Box 1: Assisted Dying for the Terminally Ill Bill (HL) 2005

Subject to the provisions of this Act, it shall be lawful for:
(a) a physician to assist a patient who is a qualifying patient to die:
(i) by prescribing such medicine, and
(ii) in the case of a patient for whom it is impossible or inappropriate orally to ingest that medication, by prescribing and providing such means of self-administration of that medication, as will enable the patient to end his own life, and
(b) a person who is a member of a healthcare team to work in conjunction with a physician to whom paragraph (a) of this section applies.
(House of Lords 2005a)

Box 2: Death tourism

The UK prohibition of euthanasia and assisted suicide has led to individuals making well-publicised trips to Switzerland for this purpose. In January 2006, Dr Anne Turner, who had progressive supranuclear palsy, travelled to Switzerland where, with the assistance of the Swiss charity Dignitas, she was given a lethal dose of barbiturates with which to end her life. Shortly before her death Dr Turner stated: 'I think it's dreadful that somebody like myself has to go to Switzerland to do this' (Boseley and Dyer 2006). Dr Turner's case reflected those of others, such as Reginald Crew, who in 2003 also used the services of Dignitas to assist him to die (MacInnes 2003).

of 'double-effect', see the second article in this series (Gallagher and Wainwright 2007).

In recent years, changes to the law have been considered on a number of occasions. In 1993/1994, a House of Lords Select Committee on Medical Ethics reviewed the law on euthanasia and concluded that it should not be legalised (House of Lords 1994). In 2003, Lord Joffe

Practising active euthanasia would usually make an individual liable to be charged with murder

introduced a private member's bill (House of Lords 2003) that progressed only to a second reading. In 2004 and 2005, Lord Joffe introduced further bills, both entitled Assisted Dying for the Terminally Ill Bill (House of Lords 2004, 2005a). The first of these sought to legalise physician-assisted suicide and voluntary euthanasia and was extensively examined by a select committee. The 2005 bill was aimed solely at introducing legislation that would allow physician-assisted suicide (Box 1). It received its second reading in May 2006 when the Lords voted (148 to 100) to delay a second reading by six months, and it therefore failed to proceed to the next stage. Lord Joffe stated his intention to reintroduce the bill in the next session of Parliament: '...and I will continue to do so until a full debate through all the usual stages has been held' (Lords *Hansard* 2006).

The Joffe bills were aimed at revising the law in England and Wales. In Scotland in 2005, Jeremy Purvis MSP undertook a consultation which invited views on a draft proposal for a Scottish Bill to 'allow capable adults with a terminal illness to access the means to die with dignity' (Purvis 2005a). He received more than 600 responses to his consultation and reported that 56 per cent of respondents were in general support of physician-assisted suicide and a change in the law (Purvis 2005b).

Should the law be changed?

Parliamentary activity in England and Scotland has increased public awareness of euthanasia and assisted suicide. In addition, widely-publicised cases such as that of Mrs Pretty (*Pretty v United Kingdom [European Court of Human Rights 2002]*) and the emergence of what has been termed 'death tourism' (Revill 2002) (Box 2), have generated much public debate, including calls for the law to be reviewed to enable individuals to exercise greater control over their own life and (ultimately) death (Annetts 2003).

Whether or not public opinion is for or against changing the law is uncertain. In 2005, it was reported that 'it is evident that there is much sympathy at a personal level for the concept of legally releasing those wishing to die from their pain and those willing to help them from legal consequences' (House of Lords 2005b).

However, it has been claimed that a lack of explanatory context undermines the findings of most surveys of public opinion on this issue: 'They are generally based on answers to "yes/no" or "either/or" questions without any explanatory context and without other options, for example, good quality palliative care, being offered. Most people have little understanding of the complexities and dangers in changing the law in this way and opinion research consists therefore to a large extent of knee-jerk answers to emotive – and often leading – questions' (Care NOT Killing 2006).

Given the complexity of the issues, it is arguable whether a true measure of public attitudes to euthanasia

has been developed. It is unrealistic simply to ask 'Are you in favour of legalising euthanasia?' and expect to extrapolate a meaningful reflection of public opinion from the responses received. To expose the range and depth of opinions relevant to such a sensitive topic would necessitate a carefully considered empirical study that investigated personal values (on a range of issues), cultural and religious influences, familiarity with the topic and personal experiences. It would be a challenging undertaking. However uncertain the findings of surveys, they undoubtedly influence the political agenda regarding euthanasia.

Opponents of euthanasia often cite the 'slippery slope' argument that legalising voluntary euthanasia would inevitably lead to the legalisation of other forms

---

Proponents of euthanasia generate prominent headlines (Evans 2006) although the dramatic emphasis given to some media reports can be misleading. For example, in 2006, a survey of 857 UK doctors found that of nearly 600,000 deaths in the UK in 2004, 0.16% (936) were a result of 'voluntary euthanasia' – although the term was used to cover such events as withholding treatment in cases when it is supposedly in the best interest of the patient. A total of 0.33% (1,930) of deaths involved 'non-voluntary euthanasia'. This was subsequently reported under the headline 'Euthanasia: doctors aid 3,000 deaths' (Boseley 2006). However, it is questionable whether any of the recorded deaths resulted from 'euthanasia' in the sense that the doctor in question actively intervened to end the patient's life.

Those who oppose a change in the law attract fewer headlines. Opponents of euthanasia often cite the 'slippery slope' argument that legalising voluntary euthanasia would inevitably lead to the legalisation of other forms of euthanasia or that non-voluntary or even involuntary euthanasia would start to occur under the guise of legalised voluntary euthanasia. According to Grayling (2001), the chief anti-euthanasia argument is that 'murder might lurk under the cloak of kindness'. Generally, the anti-euthanasia viewpoint is exposed only when a change in the law is recommended, either in parliament, the media or at prominent professional gatherings (Hall 2006, Phillips 2006).

The debate can be particularly emotive. Campaigners frequently illustrate the possible benefits (or risks) of legalising euthanasia with accounts of people for whom the current law is unsatisfactory (those who wish for assistance to die) or for whom the law currently offers protection (those who fear being killed by health professionals or being pressured into requesting legalised euthanasia). Although compelling, such emotional appeals purposely exploit individual stories to promote a pro or anti-euthanasia viewpoint and may consequently serve to discourage a balanced ethical approach to these complex issues. It is vital that health professionals impartially examine such emotionally charged and biased

Box 3: Non-UK jurisdictions

⇨ **Oregon:** The US State of Oregon Death with Dignity Act 1994 decriminalised physician-assisted suicide (it is legal in a physician-related context only), but does not allow voluntary euthanasia. The act applies only to adults who have been diagnosed with a terminal illness. A doctor provides the patient with a prescription for the fatal dose of barbiturates, the patient can then obtain the drugs when he or she chooses.

⇨ **Belgium:** The Belgian Act on Euthanasia 2002 decriminalised voluntary euthanasia (but not assisted suicide) if a physician follows pre-conditions foreseen by the law. These include that the request should be 'voluntary, well-considered and repeated'.

⇨ **Netherlands:** Physician-assisted suicide and voluntary euthanasia were decriminalised in 1991 and legalised (in a medical context only) via the Termination of Life on Request and Assisted Suicide (Review Procedures) Act 2002. The individual requesting either euthanasia or assisted suicide does not have to be terminally ill.

⇨ **Switzerland:** Both physician-assisted suicide and voluntary euthanasia are forbidden. However, Swiss law allows one individual to assist the suicide of another providing it is done for altruistic reasons, that is, the Swiss Penal Code exempts from prosecution those who assist in another's suicide if they act from entirely honourable motives, such as assisting in the suicide of a person who is suffering unbearably from illness.

In each of these jurisdictions, any act of voluntary euthanasia or assisted suicide must be recorded and reported to the relevant authorities.

reports and make practical decisions that seek to acknowledge all points of view.

To promote critical and informed debate it is essential that both sides of the argument are carefully considered and understood. The two-volume report of the 2004 House of Lords Select Committee (House of Lords 2005b) that summarises the evidence given to the committee and sets out its recommendations, provides a clear and comprehensive overview of the issues. The issues are also effectively exposed in the websites of two prominent, but opposing, groups:

⇨ Care NOT Killing (www.carenotkilling.org.uk) seeks to promote more and better palliative care, and to oppose moves to legalise assisted suicide and euthanasia.

⇨ The pro-euthanasia group Dignity in Dying, formerly the Voluntary Euthanasia Society (www.dignityindying.org.uk), claims that a change in the law will give terminally ill people more control at the end of life and enable people to keep living longer than they might otherwise have done.

18 January 2007

⇨ The above information is reprinted with kind permission from the *Nursing Standard*, the UK's bestselling nursing journal. Visit www.nursing-standard.co.uk for more.

© *Nursing Standard*

Abuse of physician assisted suicide

Respondents were asked: 'Parliament is currently debating a Bill which would allow doctors to prescribe and administer lethal drugs to patients who wish to commit suicide. If this Bill becomes law, do you think the following statement would be true? "It would make it more difficult to detect rogue doctors such as Dr Harold Shipman".'
Results by age group.

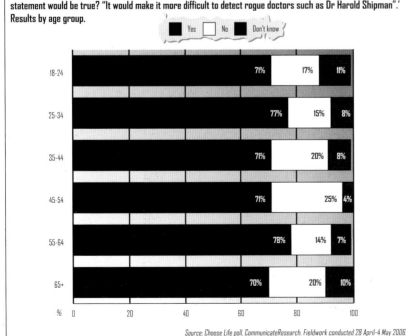

Age group	Yes	No	Don't know
18-24	71%	17%	11%
25-34	77%	15%	8%
35-44	71%	20%	8%
45-54	71%	25%	4%
55-64	78%	14%	7%
65+	70%	20%	10%

Source: Choose Life poll, CommunicateResearch. Fieldwork conducted 28 April-4 May 2006.

Legal status of euthanasia around the world

Information from Reuters

A French doctor and nurse went on trial on Monday accused of killing a terminally ill patient. They say it was a mercy killing and their supporters are demanding that France changes its laws and legalises euthanasia.

Euthanasia is an assisted death carried out directly by a doctor

Here are some facts about the legal status of euthanasia and assisted suicide.

Euthanasia – what is it?

⇨ Euthanasia is an assisted death carried out directly by a doctor; assisted suicides are those in which a deadly dose may be prescribed by the doctor or, as in Switzerland, obtained by a third party, but taken by the individual.

Where is it legal?

Netherlands

⇨ In April 2002, euthanasia became legal in the Netherlands, the first country to permit assisted deaths for the terminally ill who are desperate to die.

⇨ Opponents drew fearful parallels with Nazi Germany when the Dutch parliament voted in 2001 to enshrine in law a practice the Netherlands has tolerated for two decades.

Belgium

⇨ In May 2002, Belgium became the second country to decriminalise euthanasia.

Switzerland

⇨ Switzerland has allowed assisted suicide since the 1940s, but it was in December 2005 that a hospital allowed the procedure to take place there rather than at the home of the terminally ill patients.

⇨ Swiss law clearly decriminalises assisted suicide without the involvement of a doctor; this means that non-physicians can participate in assisted suicide.

⇨ But euthanasia, for instance when a doctor gives a patient a lethal injection on the patient's request, is not legal.

⇨ Many terminally ill foreigners travel to Switzerland to commit suicide, taking advantage of the Swiss rules which are among the world's most liberal on suicide.

United States – Oregon

⇨ The US Supreme Court ruling in January 2006 backing an Oregon law allowing doctors to help terminally ill patients to die provides legal backing that supporters hoped would spread. Assisted suicide has been allowed in Oregon since 1997.

Australia

⇨ Australia's outback Northern Territory became the first place in the world to legalise voluntary euthanasia in 1996. But the federal government vetoed the law in 1997 after four terminally ill patients had taken their own lives.

12 March 2007

⇨ The above information is reprinted with kind permission from Reuters news agency. Please visit their website at www.reuters.com for more information.

© *Reuters*

Assisted suicide and disabled people

A briefing paper from Disability Awareness in Action

Our society today is increasingly seeing impairment, disability and ageing as facets of life to be avoided at all costs. We are also a society that, because of medical advances, have grown less and less used to pain and suffering. We expect the medical profession to find a solution to any problem that we may have. Death is an infrequent visitor to families as we live longer and are more likely to survive birth and maternity. Advances in the genetic sciences send out copious messages that we can have impairment-free children, that it is quite all right to throw away embryos that have genes that may lead to disabling impairments, that we will get rid of ageing and that we will soon be able to alter genes so that all problems will be solved.

We also live with the reality. The medical profession is not infallible and many people do not receive the treatment that they should and do suffer pain and indignity. Disabled people do not have enough support, either financial or personal, and many live highly restricted, solitary and poverty-stricken lives. Television shows us pictures of these horrors daily. Soap operas turn the reality into drama, so that even if we do not have direct experience of a horrible situation, we know what it is like (or think we do). The media also concentrate on negative images of disabled and old people – on the suffering, the isolation etc. They continually make programmes in which disabled people or older people are either overcoming their tragedy or shown as useless and in need of care and protection or a danger to society and should be locked up.

And one of the greatest messages that comes from our society today is that if you are a disabled person, or a sick person or an older person – you have lost your autonomy – you can no longer have control over your own life. And this is certainly the reality for disabled people, sick people and older people who have difficulty looking after themselves. There is an army of personnel who tell them what to do, where to live, when to get up, when to get food. You cannot speak for yourself, even if you can speak.

But the solution to the fear and repulsion that ageing and disability bring is not to eliminate ageing and disability but to build a society which sees the benefits that these experiences bring to the individual, their friends and family and to the wider society and ensure that society gives all the support to and protection of the rights of each and every individual, without discrimination.

Arguments for assisted suicide

⇨ People have the right to terminate their lives when they feel that their life has become intolerable and for those who cannot kill themselves by their own hand, because of their impairments, there has to be a method of supporting their wish to commit suicide.

⇨ Without legislation assisted suicide will happen anyway, in unacceptable ways such as going abroad, or putting family members and doctors in positions of illegality.

⇨ Many people have experienced watching a loved one die in pain and suffering and do not want it to happen to themselves or other loved ones.

⇨ Hospice treatment does not always work and anyway is not always available.

⇨ An unspoken argument for euthanasia, especially of the elderly and disabled people, is cost.

Arguments against

⇨ In the UK today people can commit suicide and be free from prosecution as a criminal, but the Human Rights Act 1998 says (Schedule 1, Article 2.1) that everyone's life shall be protected by law and therefore society has a duty to prevent them from doing so by trying to alleviate the situation that they find intolerable. In the situation of someone wishing to commit suicide because of pain and suffering, it is the duty of society not to help them to die but to alleviate that pain and suffering – to, as Article 3 of the HRA says, protect them from inhuman and degrading treatment.

⇨ Legislation allowing assisted suicide, however tight the controls, inevitably reinforces negative attitudes on the quality of life of disabled people. And in all those countries where assisted suicide has been in place for some time there have been reports of considerable abuse of the legislation, particularly with regard to people with learning difficulties or other conditions where the individual is unable to communicate their wishes. And, as has recently been reported in the UK media, even people with non-life-threatening conditions

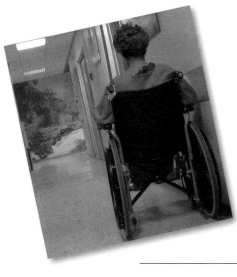

are being assisted in their suicides in Switzerland.

⇨ Another factor to consider is that many of the people in Holland who have been legally assisted to end their lives had the physical capacity to take their own lives (see published accounts from Dutch doctors who have practised assisted suicide/euthanasia). There has not been anything like enough discussion around this issue – are these suicides really taking control of their own deaths or are they handing the responsibility to someone else?

⇨ The argument that pain and suffering must be ended is un-controvertible. But this should be done through alleviation of the pain and suffering, not through ending the individual's life. The HRA does give situations where the deprivation of life would not be regarded as in contravention of Article 2.1 but only in cases of self-defence, lawful arrest, escaping detainees and quelling a riot or insurrection. 'Death with dignity' (as euthanasia is so often called by its protagonists) is not one which arises from desperation and by someone else's hand but one where the individual is truly and fully supported to make the most of what life is left to them.

⇨ There is mounting evidence that both the legal and medical professions and society in general believe that disabled people's lives are not worth living and that they should not be subject to the same criteria as non-disabled people. DNR notices are being routinely put on people's notes in hospital – especially the elderly. Parents are being told that the possibility of having a disabled child is unfair on the child and that they will have a life of pain and suffering.

⇨ Put crudely, old people and disabled people are cheaper dead than alive. This is a very real argument in today's climate of soaring health costs and is one that also underpins euthanasia of new-born babies and the information given to parents to encourage them to abort a disabled foetus (or a foetus that may have an disabling impairment).

As Dr Ian Basnett says:

'I became quadriplegic following a sporting accident 17 years ago. I was ventilator dependent for a while and at times said to people, "I wish I was dead!" I am now extraordinarily glad no one acted on that and assisted suicide was not legal. I think the first difficulty I faced was the fact that, like many people, I had a terribly negative image of disability. When you suddenly become severely disabled you still have that viewpoint. Before I was disabled, I was working as a junior doctor. That brought me into contact with disabled people and I remember clerking in a man with quadriplegia. My reaction was, how could anyone live like that? I said to my then girlfriend, "I'd rather be dead, if I couldn't play sport".'

Dr. Basnett now knows that there is more to life than sport!

By Rachel Hurst

⇨ The above information is re-printed with kind permission from Disability Awareness in Action, the international disability and human rights network. For more information, visit www.daa.org.uk

© *Disability Awareness in Action*

Fury as euthanasia group puts dignity in new name

By Sarah Womack, Social Affairs Correspondent

Plans by the Voluntary Euthanasia Society to rename itself Dignity in Dying came under bitter attack last night.

Critics said the phrase was used by terminally ill people seeking a better quality of life – not asking for euthanasia or assisted suicide.

The name change comes 71 years after the society was set up and follows research showing doctors are involved in as many as eight deaths a day from voluntary or 'non-voluntary' euthanasia.

Representatives of the disabled, and experts in medical ethics and palliative care, strongly objected to the society using Dignity in Dying. In a letter to Alan Johnson, the Trade Secretary, they said the phrase was 'used by patients worried about the care they will receive.

'These patients are not asking for euthanasia or assisted suicide; they are asking for good care.'

The signatories said at least five charities caring for the disabled and terminally ill had dignity in their names.

'If the change takes place, whenever a lecture is given in future about improved care for the dying it will broadcast an inadvertent advertisement for the VES.'

The letter was signed by John Wiles, the chairman of the Association of Palliative Medicine, Jane Campbell of Not Dead Yet UK, Tony Cole, the chairman of the Medical Ethics Alliance, Jared O'Mara of the British Council of Disabled People, and Rob George, a senior lecturer in bioethics and the philosophy of medicine.

The society, which was planning to announce its new name on Monday, said it had been received well by MPs and members of the Lords.

Deborah Annetts, the chief executive, said members had sent in about 200 suggestions for a name change, which a group of staff and members reduced to two: Choice in Dying and Dignity in Dying.

About 65 per cent of the public preferred Dignity in Dying, she said.

The VES dismissed the letter to Mr Johnson saying it was from a tiny cluster of people with pro-Roman Catholic views.

21 January 2006

© *Telegraph Group Limited, London 2006*

Palliative care

Information from Dignity in Dying

Dignity in Dying strongly supports good palliative care. We believe that all terminally ill patients should have access to good quality palliative care.

Palliative care shouldn't be perceived as an optional extra but should be a basic right for everyone. Palliative care should become part of mainstream medicine and give people appropriate relief and real choice.

Currently, insufficient resources are made available. This allows the current inequalities in accessing palliative care depending on diagnosis, age, gender or the place where people live. We fully support calls for better palliative care services.

Dignity in Dying wants to see:

⇨ A system where patients receive an individual package of care that responds to their specific needs, where their concerns and those of their relatives are being met, and where they receive physical relief, and psychological and social support.

⇨ A palliative care network that allows people to receive care, and to die, in the place of their preference. Currently, 57% of the people would prefer to die at home but only 20% do so. Only 13% would want to die in hospital but 58% of people spend the last days of their lives on a hospital ward.

⇨ An integrated model of health and social care that results in continuity of care for patients nearing the end of their lives.

⇨ A health care and social care workforce comprising of a sufficient number of specialist palliative care staff and with all staff demonstrating sufficient skills and knowledge in the area of palliative care.

Patient choice is crucial in palliative care:

⇨ Patient choice must be central to all decision-making on palliative care, with full access to good palliative care for everyone who needs it.

⇨ There needs to be sensible acknowledgement by decision-makers and health care professionals that palliative care cannot meet the needs of all dying patients, a fact acknowledged by the BMA, the NCPC and Macmillan. No amount of good palliative care can address some patients' concerns regarding their loss of autonomy, loss of dignity and loss of control. We therefore believe that patient choice should include the right to a medically assisted death for those who are terminally ill and suffer unbearably.

⇨ We believe in a society at ease with discussing issues around dying, where people get all the information they need on the options available to them, where people are encouraged to plan ahead and express their wishes about end-of-life care and discuss their preferences with their family, friends and health care professionals.

Dignity in Dying believes that this is not only possible but is necessary if we want to achieve real patient choice at the end of life.

Campaign

Dignity in Dying is campaigning for more care and more choice at the end of life. We want to see a patient-centred approach to end-of-life care which provides all appropriate options to dying patients including access to excellent palliative care and, as a last resort for those in unbearable suffering, a medically assisted death.

You can get involved by sending one of our palliative care campaign postcards to your MP. Contact James Harris on james.harris@ dignityindying.org.uk or 020 7479 7739 to order your postcard or if you have any questions about the campaign. If you are emailing James, please include your name and full postal address.

Assisted dying and palliative care

Palliative care and assisted dying are often presented as opposing forces. Some critics of assisted dying state that legislating for assisted dying could undermine developments to palliative care.

However, all the evidence from Oregon and the Netherlands demonstrates that the opposite is true – palliative care has continued to grow and develop since assisted dying was made legal.

⇨ The above information is reprinted with kind permission from Dignity in Dying. Visit www.dignityindying.org. uk for more information.

© *Dignity in Dying*

How common is euthanasia?

British doctors use euthanasia to kill nearly 3,000 patients

A new survey finds British doctors used euthanasia to kill nearly 3,000 patients in 2004. The poll also found that British doctors do not want to see the legalisation of assisted suicide despite a campaign to do that.

Brunel University surveyed 857 doctors and found that thousands of deaths in 2004 were the result of illegal euthanasia.

> ### Brunel University surveyed 857 doctors and found that thousands of deaths in 2004 were the result of illegal euthanasia

According to a BBC report, the survey found that, of the 584,791 deaths in the UK in 2004, 936 were by voluntary euthanasia and 1,930 involved the doctor killing the patient without the patient's consent.

By Steven Ertelt, LifeNews.com Editor

Of the euthanasia deaths, one-third of them were the result of doctors treating the symptoms of a disease or injury and just under a third involved doctors withholding treatment in cases when it is supposedly in the best interest of the patient.

Both of those courses of action are legal in Britain, the BBC reported.

None of the doctors in the poll said they had been involved in an assisted suicide and just 2.6 percent of the physicians surveyed said it would be beneficial to change the law to allow it.

Discussing the report, Professor Clive Seale told the BBC, 'Euthanasia and physician-assisted suicide are understandably very emotive subjects, but this work shows that UK doctors are less willing to take such actions than in several other countries.'

In November lawmakers in the House of Lords introduced a private member's bill to legalise assisted suicide. Pro-life groups have strenuously fought the bill and were successful in getting a provision allowing voluntary euthanasia to be removed from it.

Groups backing euthanasia said the report shows some doctors are engaging in the practice and that it should be legalised, but pro-life advocates disagreed.

Julia Millington, political director of the ProLife Alliance, told the BBC, 'Surely the response of a civilised society is to stop this unlawful killing altogether rather than use such research to support demands for doctors to be permitted to do it legally.'

A doctor associated with the British Medical Association also worried about the number of doctors engaging in euthanasia.

17 January 2006

⇨ The above information is reprinted with kind permission from LifeNews.com. Visit www.lifenews. com for more, or view this article at www.lifenews.com/bio1280.html

© *LifeNews.com*

Euthanasia: a doctor's viewpoint

Results of first ever UK-wide study into euthanasia and end-of-life decisions

The results of the first UK-wide study into euthanasia are revealed today in *Palliative Medicine*. The survey, carried out by a Brunel University academic, shows the proportion of UK deaths in which doctors report having assisted patients' suicide, carried out euthanasia, or taken other medical decisions relating to the ending of life. This is the first time such a comprehensive survey of UK medical practice has been reported. Because the same survey has been done in other countries, rates in the UK can be compared with rates elsewhere.

Results overview

Right to die: According to the results, there are no incidences of physician-assisted suicide in the UK. Incidences of voluntary euthanasia and ending of life without an explicit request from a patient (both of which are illegal practices) were reported, however, both of these occur significantly less frequently than in most of the other countries where the survey has been carried out.

Law in the way: A small proportion of the 857 doctors who replied to the survey felt UK law had inhibited or interfered with their preferred management of the patient on whose care they reported (4.6% of doctors) or that a new law would have facilitated better management of that patient (2.6% of doctors).

Support for ban: 51 doctors wrote comments on the questionnaires containing views about the desirability of legal change or of medical involvement in hastening death. The majority of these (82%) supported the current legal ban on medical involvement in euthanasia or assisted suicide.

857 medical practitioners responded to the anonymous survey, providing details on the last death they attended. The doctors' replies were used to estimate the proportion of UK deaths where particular end-of-life decisions were made. The proportion of UK deaths involving an end-of-life decision were:

Percentage of instances as proportion of total UK deaths

⇨ (1) voluntary euthanasia: 0.16%
⇨ (2) physician-assisted suicide: 0.00%
⇨ (3) ending of life without an explicit request from patient: 0.33%
⇨ (4) alleviation of symptoms with possibly life-shortening effect: 32.8%
⇨ (5) 'non-treatment' decisions (e.g.: withholding or withdrawing treatment): 30.3%

(1) and (2) were significantly less frequent in the UK than in the Netherlands and Australia.

(2) was also less frequent in the UK than Switzerland.

(3) was less frequent in the UK than in Belgium and Australia.

Comparison of UK and New Zealand general practitioners showed lower rates of (4) and (5) in the UK.

(5) was more common in the UK than in most other European countries.

The author of the report, Clive Seale, Professor of Sociology at Brunel University, West London, comments: 'This is the first time a nationally representative survey of end-of-life decisions taken by doctors in the UK has been done and it has produced some interesting results. Euthanasia and physician-assisted suicide are understandably very emotive subjects, but this work shows that UK doctors are less willing to take such actions than in several other countries. We have a very strong ethos of providing excellent palliative care in the UK, reflected in the finding that doctors in the UK are willing to make other kinds of decisions that prioritise the comfort of patients, without striving to preserve life at the cost of suffering. The results suggest that providing the best kind of patient care is a major driver behind medical decision making.'

Notes

How the survey was conducted
The study was funded by the Nuffield

Foundation and carried out by Professor Clive Seale of the School of Social Sciences and Law, Brunel University.

857 UK medical practitioners responded to a postal survey in 2004, using the same questionnaire employed by other countries. Returns were rendered anonymous using the same procedures as in other countries. This means that doctors were free to report their experiences honestly, and results are comparable with other countries where the survey has been done. Each doctor reported in detail on the last death they had attended.

The responses were then compared with the results of similar surveys conducted in the Netherlands, Australia, New Zealand, Belgium,

Italy, Denmark, Sweden and Switzerland.

General statistics

⇨ In 2004 there were 584,791 deaths in England, Wales, Scotland and Northern Ireland.

⇨ The Assisted Dying for the Terminally Ill Bill, sponsored by Lord Joffe, was debated in the House of Lords in October 2005.

⇨ The British Medical Association voted in its 2005 annual meeting to drop its resistance to a change in the law on assisted suicide and adopt a stance of neutrality, making it a matter for society to decide.

⇨ To date various forms of medically assisted dying that are currently illegal in the UK (for example,

euthanasia or physician-assisted suicide) have been legalised in countries such as the Netherlands, Belgium, Switzerland and Oregon, USA.

Full source of the research

Seale, C. (2006) National survey of end-of-life decisions made by UK medical practitioners. *Palliative Medicine* 20: 1-8. For further information on the publication, please visit: http://www. arnoldpublishers.com/journals/ pages/pal_med/02692163.htm *17 January 2006*

⇨ The above information is reprinted with kind permission from Brunel University, West London. Visit www. brunel.ac.uk for more information.

© *Brunel University, West London*

Majority of GPs 'stop treating terminally ill'

More than half of GPs have withheld treatment from terminally ill patients knowing it could hasten death, a survey published yesterday suggested.

The study of more than 300 family doctors, by *Pulse* magazine, found that 54 per cent had held back drugs such as antibiotics. Almost four out of five – 79 per cent – believe there are circumstances when such action is justified.

Thirty per cent of those surveyed thought physician-assisted suicide should be legalised and 42 per cent would be prepared to help a patient die if the law was changed.

Almost three in five of GPs questioned, 58 per cent, had given pain-relief drugs which might hasten death, even if that was not the intended consequence. Three-quarters said this could be justified.

Deborah Annetts, the chief executive of Dignity in Dying, said: 'This survey shows what we have long said – that doctors hold a range of views on assisted dying and that many support a change in the law.

'It shows that GPs are in touch with the views of the vast majority of their patients – 80 per cent of the

By Nic Fleming, Medical Correspondent

public believe that a terminally ill person should have the option of an assisted death.

'Given the range of views held by doctors on this issue, it is a shame the organisations that are supposed to represent them are failing to do so, and on an issue of such great importance to the public.'

In the past 18 months, the British Medical Association and the Royal

Colleges of Physicians and of GPs have all changed their position on euthanasia from neutrality to opposition.

A spokesman for the BMA said: 'This is a very sensitive issue and doctors have varying views on it. Our position is we are opposed to physician-assisted suicide. At the moment, the majority of doctors are opposed.

'There is a very clear moral and legal distinction between knowing that a treatment may cause harm and deliberately intending to kill a patient.'

DOCTOR   PATIENT

'If a doctor's intention is to relieve pain and distress they will not have broken the law.'

More than half of GPs have withheld treatment from terminally ill patients knowing it could hasten death

The results suggested that younger GPs were more supportive of assisted suicide than colleagues over 65, although the number of older doctors surveyed was small.

Dr Peter Jolliffe, the chief executive of Devon local medical committee, which represents GPs and GP practices, said: 'My personal view would be there are times in life where suicide is a perfectly logical, sensible and understandable thing to do.

'If society is going to go down that route I don't see that it would have to be a doctor who administered the pill or gave the injection – I would find it difficult to do so.'

Dr Peter Saunders, campaign director of the Care NOT Killing Alliance, said: 'It is quite appropriate to withhold treatment such as antibiotics when death is imminent and inevitable and when the burden of giving them outweighs any benefit.

'There is a huge difference between withholding treatment with the intention of hastening death, which is unethical, and withholding treatment in the knowledge that death may be hastened.

'The *Pulse* survey reflects the fact that many GPs mistakenly believe that you can't kill the pain without killing the patient. Morphine, properly used, does not hasten death.'

19 May 2007

© *Telegraph Group Limited, London 2007*

Morphine kills pain not patients

Information from Care NOT Killing

Morphine is a safe and effective painkiller and should never cause death, according to a major new study which explodes the myth that doctors use the drug to hasten the end for terminally ill patients.

The new research comes in the wake of controversy around the case of Kelly Taylor, a 30-year-old woman with Eisenmenger's syndrome, who is currently seeking legal permission to be heavily sedated with morphine and then dehydrated until she dies.

A speaker on Radio Four's *Thought for Today*, the Revd Alan Billings, Director of the Centre for Ethics and Religion at Lancaster University, courted controversy last week by commenting on the case and implying that morphine frequently ends the lives of terminally ill people, and causes sedation when given in doses necessary to relieve pain.

Commenting on the new research, Andrew Thorns, Chair of the Ethics Committee of the Association for Palliative Medicine representing 800 UK palliative medicine doctors, said: 'Morphine is a safe and effective pain-killer. It should never be necessary to give such high doses of morphine for pain that the patient dies as a result.

'Only in massive overdose would this be the case and this should never be the intention of any doctor. Research and clinical practice shows that good symptom control involves far more than simply prescribing medication and can be achieved without the risk of shortening life. The dose of morphine should be adjusted to meet the individual patient's pain requirements, with the aim of allowing the person to be free of pain without the development of unwanted side-effects.'

The study by Estfan and Colleagues at the Taussig Cancer Clinic in Cleveland, USA, is published today in the leading medical journal, *Palliative Medicine*, and involved 30 patients with severe cancer pain.

It demonstrates clearly that when prescribed properly in patients with severe pain, opioids drugs like morphine do not cause respiratory depression. There were no significant changes in objective measures of respiration such as oxygen saturation and CO2 before and after the pain was controlled.

Rob George, London Consultant in Palliative Medicine, commented: 'Doctors in palliative care are never faced with the dilemma of controlling severe pain at the risk of killing the patient. They manage pain with drugs and doses adjusted to

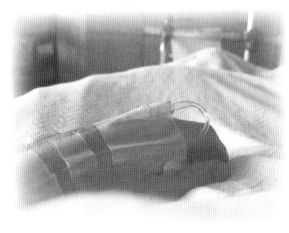

individual patients so that they can be comfortable and able to live with dignity until they die.

'It is most regrettable that the truth about morphine's safety and efficacy never appears in the general press while claims about the so-called double effect, euthanasia and doctors "killing" with morphine automatically do.'

In the same edition of the journal, George and Regnard, in a commentary on the research, highlight the erroneous linkage between morphine and the so-called 'Double Effect'.

They point out that, unlike many other drugs, morphine and other opioids have a very wide safety margin; that evidence over the last 20 years has repeatedly shown that, used correctly, morphine is well tolerated, does not cloud the mind, does not shorten life, and its sedating effects wear off quickly. In fact, inappropriately high, toxic doses may cause agitation

and distress rather than respiratory compromise.

Dr George added: 'When correctly used to relieve pain in a patient who is terminally ill, morphine-like drugs should never cause death. By contrast they may well lengthen life and certainly improve its quality.

'Our key priority must be to ensure that the public are properly informed about the safety of pain and symptom control and to make the best palliative care more widely accessible. We need to overcome the postcode lottery of palliative care that currently exists in this country.'

The new research also comes in the wake of Baroness Ilora Finlay's Palliative Care Bill, which seeks to make good quality palliative care more widely accessible in England and Wales. This bill had an unopposed second reading in the House of Lords on Friday 23 February. It will now proceed to a Committee of the Whole House and thence to a Third

Reading. If it passes a Third Reading, then it will proceed to the House of Commons, but only if it is granted time by the Government.

Dr George concluded, 'We call on the Government to make time for this landmark bill, in order to ensure that all terminally ill patients in the UK benefit from the very best care available.'

The Ethics Committee of the Association for Palliative Medicine (APM) represents an organisation of over 800 palliative medicine doctors working in hospices, hospitals and the community across England, Ireland, Scotland and Wales. The APM is a member of Care NOT Killing.
1 March 2007

⇨ The above information is reprinted with kind permission from Care NOT Killing. Visit www.carenotkilling.org.uk for more information.

© Care NOT Killing

Should we legalise euthanasia?

Euthanasia should not be legalised, say two-thirds of GPs

More than two-thirds of GPs still oppose the legalisation of euthanasia, a survey has revealed.

Even if they were allowed to do so, less than half – 42 per cent – would be prepared to help a terminally-ill patient die.

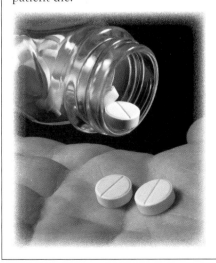

By Daniel Martin

However, the survey, by GPs' magazine *Pulse*, shows that many doctors had taken actions which may have hastened a patient's death.

The survey of 309 GPs found that more than half – 54 per cent – had withheld treatment such as antibiotics to a patient, knowing it could hasten their death.

Four in five said that whether or not they had done so themselves, such a decision could be justified.

And 58 per cent had given pain-relieving drugs which could hasten death, even if that was not the intended consequence. Three-quarters said that could be justified.

A spokeswoman for the Pro-Life Alliance said: 'We welcome the results of this poll, which reflects the strength

of opposition to euthanasia within the medical profession.

'Opposition to the legalisation of physician-assisted suicide and euthanasia has been repeatedly affirmed in the policies adopted by various medical bodies.

'It is perfectly acceptable for doctors to use their discretion to withhold medical treatment when such treatment is futile and will be a burden rather than a benefit to the patient. This is not euthanasia.'

Dr Peter Saunders of the Care NOT Killing Alliance, said: 'It is striking that so many justify doses of painkilling medicine to hasten death.

'It illustrates the huge number of GPs who don't understand how to use painkilling drugs such as morphine properly.

'The priority has to be to make good palliative care more widely acceptable and train the vast number of ignorant GPs about the proper use of morphine.'

80 per cent of the public believe that a terminally-ill person should have the option of an assisted death

Dignity in Dying chief executive Deborah Annetts said: 'This survey clearly shows what Dignity in Dying has long said: that doctors hold a range of views on assisted dying and that many support a change in the law.

'*Pulse* magazine's survey demonstrates that GPs are in touch with the views of the vast majority of their patients: 80 per cent of the public believe that a terminally-ill person should have the option of an assisted death.

'Given the range of views held by doctors on this issue, it is a shame the organisations that are supposed to represent them are failing to do so, and on an issue of such great importance to the public.'

She added: 'This survey is yet another signal that the medical associations are out of step with doctors and the public.'

Members of the British Medical Association voted last year to oppose euthanasia and physician-assisted suicide. It overturned a decision made the previous year to adopt a neutral position towards so-called mercy killings.

A spokeswoman said: 'The BMA has members with wide-ranging views on these issues but at last year's annual meeting the majority of doctors voted to oppose any form of assisted dying.

'The BMA will continue to debate this subject and represent the views of its members.'

⇨ This article first appeared in the *Daily Mail*, 18 May 2007.

© 2007 Associated Newspapers Ltd

Call for euthanasia legislation

Legalise non-voluntary euthanasia, says professor of medical ethics

One of the UK's leading medical ethicists, Emeritus Professor Len Doyal, has called for the legalisation of voluntary and non-voluntary euthanasia in Britain.

Writing in the Royal Society of Medicine's *Clinical Ethics* journal, Professor Doyal said, 'Doctor assisted deaths are taking place on a regular and recurring basis in the UK. They should be better regulated.'

'When doctors withdraw life-sustaining treatment such as feeding tubes from severely incompetent patients, it should morally be recognised for what it is – euthanasia where death is foreseen with certainty.

'Doctors may not want to admit this and couch their decision in terms such as "alleviating suffering" but withdrawal of life sustaining treatment from severely incompetent patients is morally equivalent to active euthanasia,' he stated.

Professor Doyal asked, 'If doctors can already choose not to keep uncomprehending patients alive because they believe that life is of no further benefit to them, why should their death be needlessly prolonged?

'It is ironic that much of the debate about euthanasia has been so focused on competent patients. Withdrawing feeding tubes, ventilators or antibiotics from incompetent patients may result in a slow, painful and incomprehensible death that could be avoided through the legalisation of non-voluntary active euthanasia.'

Referring specifically to the Joffe Bill, Professor Doyal claimed, 'Some supporters of euthanasia remain silent about non-voluntary euthanasia, presumably because they believe that focusing on voluntary euthanasia offers a better chance of legalisation. Yet in doing so, they ignore important arguments for their own position.

'If doctors are now allowed control – and should be able to exert even more control – over the deaths of severely incompetent patients, why should competent patients not be able to control the circumstances of their own deaths if this is what they wish?

'Proponents of voluntary euthanasia should support non-voluntary euthanasia under appropriate circumstances and with proper regulation,' Professor Doyal concluded.

Notes

Len Doyal is Emeritus Professor of Medical Ethics at Barts and the London School of Medicine and Dentistry, Queen Mary, University of London. Professor Doyal lectures, publishes and consults widely. He has been a member of the BMA Ethics Committee for nine years.

⇨ The above information is reprinted with kind permission from the Royal Society. Visit http://royalsociety.org for more information.

© Royal Society

Physician-assisted suicide

Information from Religious Tolerance

Activities in England, Wales and Scotland

⇨ 8 December 1999: According to Maranatha Daywatch: 'A British charity Monday called for a government inquiry into claims that health officials are practising "involuntary euthanasia" on elderly patients in an attempt to free up beds in overcrowded hospitals. Age Concern accused the National Health Service (NHS) of "ageism" and called on the Labour government to keep a pre-election promise to tackle the problem of neglect of older patients.'[1] There are allegations that elderly patients are being deprived of food and water. A second pressure group, Patients in Danger, is considering charging the government in the European Court of Human Rights.

⇨ April 2000: Anti-euthanasia bill defeated: An anti-euthanasia bill was defeated in Parliament. Dr Liam Fox, spokesperson for the Conservative Party, expressed alarm at the status of passive euthanasia in England. The party is concerned that orders have been issued that at least 50 patients be allowed to die and not be resuscitated when their breathing or heart stops. The party is calling for clear guidelines to medical personnel.

⇨ 1 August 2004: Assisted suicide being studied:
  ↪ England and Wales: A select committee on medical ethics of the House of Lords is conducted hearings on Lord Joffe's Patient (Assisted Dying) Bill. Information is being supplied by a group of campaigners, health professionals and organisations. If the bill is passed, it would legalise physician-assisted suicide in England and Wales. The Royal College of Nurs-

ing is taking a poll of its members for the first time.
  ↪ Scotland: Jeremy Purvis, a Liberal Democrat in Scotland, is drafting a bill to legalise 'mercy killing'. He is basing the bill on the existing law in Oregon. He said: 'It's a very sensitive issue and I believe we should be having a debate about this in Scotland. If a draft bill would stimulate that then I would be looking to give notice to put one down. I've been looking in a lot of detail at the Oregon experience. What struck me was when the patients made the request to their doctor for physician-assisted suicide, they did so because they wanted to have dignity at the end...It's very important that we are affording people choices in life to an ever greater extent.'

Purvis said: 'The select committee in the Lords will be gathering considerable evidence and I don't think it will be necessarily helpful to duplicate that. But there are differences in English and Scottish law and that is why I think it would be better if the debate was taken forward in Scotland.'

The news of the bill was welcomed by pro-choice groups and some politicians. It was condemned by the Roman Catholic Church:

⇨ Jenny Saunders, a spokesperson for the Voluntary Euthanasia Society, said: 'The current law doesn't prevent assisted dying, it simply makes this practice dangerous by forcing it to happen behind closed doors where there are no safeguards...It is vitally important assisted dying is brought into the open, so that parliament can introduce regulation to better protect the terminally ill, medical staff and vulnerable people.'

⇨ Carol Stewart, of the Disability Rights Commission Scotland, said: 'I would be concerned that a bill would not afford disabled people protection from having decisions imposed upon them. That must not be allowed to happen.'

⇨ Peter Kearney, a spokesperson for the Roman Catholic Church in Scotland, said: 'If the issue was debated we would come out very clearly against euthanasia. It's fraught with dangers. It would give a licence for the legalised killing of people, possibly against their will.' The church appears to be unaware of the law in Oregon upon which this bill is based. That law requires the patient to take the initiative in requesting help in dying.

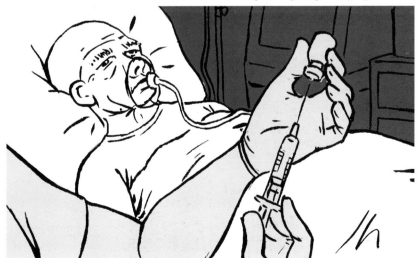

➪ 3 September 2004: Euthanasia group has helped 22 Britons to die: There is a ban on assisted suicide in the UK. However, a Swiss-based group, Dignitas, has helped 22 residents of Britain to commit suicide in the face of extreme suffering. Dignitas was organised in 1998 to help people with chronic diseases to 'die with dignity'. They have assisted 304 people to commit suicide, about 200 of whom were from outside Switzerland. They have 557 members in the UK. Mark Slattery of the Voluntary Euthanasia Society said: 'The British law is less liberal and more restrictive than other western European countries. That means we are more likely to seek assistance overseas.'[2] There are problems with this arrangement. First the person seeking to die must somehow make it to Switzerland. This may be a very difficult undertaking if the person is very seriously ill. Second, the spouse or family member or friend accompanying the individual is exposing themselves to prosecution when they return to the UK. The government's Crown Prosecution Service has sometimes taken a long time to decide whether to prosecute the helper: eight months in one case. Meanwhile, Swiss authorities are considering making foreigners wait six months, often in intractable pain, before they can use Dignitas, in an attempt to stop what they call 'suicide tourism.'[3]

➪ 12 December 2005: Scotland: Private member's bill fails: Jeremy Purvis initiated a private member's bill in the Scottish Parliament '... to allow for a mentally capable, terminally ill adult the right to receive medical assistance to die'. By mid December, it had not received the minimum of 18 supporters that would have allowed it to proceed. One reason for this lack of support might be the upcoming 2007 election. There was such a massive outpouring of opposition at the time of 'Section 28' – a regulation governing the teaching of homosexuality in schools – that Parliament members did not want to inflame the electorate at this time.[4]

➪ 31 January 2006: New alliance formed to promote palliative care and oppose PAS: Care NOT Killing, a new alliance of 21 organisations was formed to promote palliative care and oppose euthanasia. Members of the alliance include the Association of Palliative Medicine, the British Council of Disabled People, RADAR, the Christian Medical Fellowship and the Medical Ethics Alliance. Memberships are available to both groups and individuals who support their cause. The launch was featured on BBC breakfast TV, the Radio Four *Today* programme, Radio Five Live and the BBC health pages.[5]

➪ 12 May 2006: House of Lords blocks private member's bill: Following an intense seven-hour debate, the House of Lords voted to block a bill that would have given terminally ill persons the right to assisted suicide. The vote was 148 to 100.

➪ Dr Rowan Williams, the Archbishop of Canterbury said that: 'Opposition to the principle of this Bill is not confined to people of religious conviction...Whether or not you believe that God enters into the consideration, it remains true that to specify even in the fairly broad terms of this Bill conditions under which it would be both reasonable and legal to end your life, is to say that certain kinds of life are not worth living.'

➪ Lord Joffe said that a solution must be found 'to the unbearable suffering of patients whose needs cannot be met by palliative care. As a caring society we cannot sit back and complacently accept that terminally ill patients suffering unbearably should just continue to suffer for the good of society as a whole.'[6,7]

➪ 17 May 2006: Motion in the House of Commons: A motion was made: 'That this House is saddened by the death of the terminally ill doctor Anne Turner who chose to travel to Switzerland to receive assistance to die; hopes that her son and daughters who accompanied her are treated with compassion and sensitivity by the authorities on their return to the UK; is concerned that this is the 42nd case of its kind in the past three years and yet the Director of Public Prosecutions still refuses to publish guidance as to whether family members who accompany their relatives overseas for an assisted death are breaking the law; notes that recent research by Clive Seale from Brunel University has uncovered that, on average, there are eight illegal assisted deaths performed by doctors in the UK every day; and believes this sensitive issue should be further discussed in this House.'

References

1 Maranatha Christian Journal is a religious online news source at: http://www.mcjonline.com. Their article on euthanasia is at: http://www.mcjonline.com

2 Liam McDougall, 'Holyrood braces itself for Scottish euthanasia bill,' Sunday Herald Online, 1 August 2001, at: http://www.sundayherald.com/

3 Daniel Martin and Vikram Dodd, 'Euthanasia group may have helped 22 Britons die,' *The Guardian*, 3 September 2003, at: http://society.guardian.co.uk/

4 'Scottish euthanasia bill fails,' Care NOT Killing, at: http://www.carenotkilling.org.uk/

5 Care NOT Killing's website is at: http://www.carenotkilling.org.uk/

6 'Lords reject right to die bill,' *Daily Telegraph*, 12 May 2006, at: http://www.telegraph.co.uk/

7 'Assisted Dying for the Terminally Ill Bill,' House of Lords, at: http://www.publications.parliament.uk/

Author: B.A. Robinson

➪ The above information is reprinted with kind permission from Religious Tolerance. Visit www.religioustolerance.org for more information.

Study counters argument against assisted suicide

Legalising assisted suicide won't hike deaths among vulnerable, experts say

A study of doctor-assisted suicide in the Netherlands and Oregon counters the argument that making it legal may lead to more of these deaths among vulnerable groups like the disabled, although it did find some evidence for this among people with AIDS.

The research, published on Wednesday, tested the 'slippery slope' argument advanced by some critics that by permitting doctors to help certain patients end their lives, members of some groups may die in disproportionately large numbers.

They analysed data from two leading places where assisted suicide is legal and tracked 10 'vulnerable' groups, including the physically disabled, chronically ill, mentally ill, elderly, poor, racial and ethnic minorities, women and others.

Critics of assisted suicide have argued that people in these groups might be influenced to end their lives through doctor-assisted suicide.

'We found that there is no evidence of disproportionate impact of these practices, when legal, on any of those groups, with the exception of people with AIDS,' University of Utah bioethicist Margaret Battin, who led the study appearing in the *Journal of Medical Ethics*, said in a telephone interview.

The researchers looked at data on assisted suicide and euthanasia in the Netherlands from 1985 to 2005 and Oregon Department of Human Services annual reports for 1998 to 2006, along with surveys of doctors and hospice workers. Oregon is the only US state where doctor-assisted suicide is legal.

'Those who received physician-assisted dying in the jurisdictions studied appeared to enjoy comparative social, economic, educational, professional and other privileges,' the researchers wrote.

By Will Dunham

Average age of 70

About 80 per cent of those who died with a doctor's help in the Netherlands and Oregon were cancer patients. The average age for those dying via doctor-assisted suicide was 70.

> A study of doctor-assisted suicide in the Netherlands and Oregon counters the argument that making it legal may lead to more of these deaths among vulnerable groups like the disabled

The only disproportionate deaths were seen among people with AIDS, an incurable viral disease, although the actual number of these deaths was extremely small, the study found. In Oregon, only six people with AIDS died via doctor-assisted suicide in the nine years studied, the researchers said.

People with AIDS were 30 times more likely to use assisted dying than, for example, a comparable group of people who died due to chronic respiratory illnesses, the researchers said.

Oregon's law permits doctors to prescribe lethal drugs to patients who have been diagnosed by two doctors as having a terminal illness, with less than six months left to live. Patients then administer the drugs themselves.

The Netherlands allows doctors to prescribe lethal drugs for suicide or perform 'voluntary active euthanasia' in which the doctor rather than the patient administers the medication.

The 'slippery slope' argument is just one of several advanced by people who oppose this practice. Other arguments against it include protecting the sanctity of life and the integrity of doctors.

Arguments advanced by some who support doctor-assisted suicide include preventing needless pain and suffering in terminally ill patients and giving these people the right to decide their own fate as they see fit.
26 September 2007

⇨ The above information is re-printed with kind permission from Reuters news agency. Visit www.reuters.com for more information.

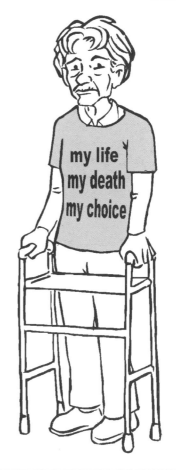

When premature babies should be allowed to die

Information from the *New Scientist*. By Gaia Vince

Struggling babies born after just 22 weeks' gestation should be allowed to die, but everything should be done to support babies born after 24 weeks, an independent ethics panel announced today.

For babies born between 23 and 24 weeks, doctors, parents and nursing staff should come to a mutual decision about whether or not to resuscitate, the researchers say.

The UK has the highest rate of low birthweight babies in western Europe

The new guidelines by the UK's Nuffield Council on Bioethics, issued on Thursday, are the culmination of two years' research into when to give intensive care to babies that are born extremely prematurely.

They make recommendations on how to deal with the issue of babies born with very low chances of survival and high risk of severe disability, as well as how to resolve conflicts between parents and medical professionals on the treatment of premature infants.

Growing chances

There are only anecdotal reports of babies surviving after fewer than 22 weeks in the womb. At that time, babies have just a 1% chance of survival with intensive care and are almost certain to suffer severe disability, the researchers say.

After 23 weeks' gestation, a baby has just a 16% chance of surviving with intensive care, and a 64% risk of serious disability. At 24 weeks, survival is 44%, but by 25 weeks, the survival rate is 63% and risk of severe disability is 40%.

'The majority of babies still die at 23 weeks and the majority have a serious disability, including illness such as cerebral palsy,' says Andrew Whitelaw, professor of neonatal medicine at the University of Bristol, UK, who helped compile the report. Prolonging the life of profoundly sick premature babies may be 'inhumane' and place an 'intolerable burden on the baby', the researchers say.

Hard choices

Such tiny babies often face as many as 50 interventions per day – everything from continual needle pricks, to having a tube in their throat, to brain surgery. The constant pain and stress that these infants face is unethical – in most cases the 'treatment just prolongs the process of dying', Whitelaw says.

The difficulty, he says, is making the decision about whether to move from treatment to palliative care, because it is not always possible to tell for months which babies will survive and thrive and which will die or be left with horrendous disabilities, he told *New Scientist*.

Currently, the situation is fairly ad hoc, with individual hospitals across the UK imposing their own criteria for when to resuscitate, says Whitelaw. In some hospitals, the policy is to not resuscitate babies born at 23 weeks or less. In others, every single baby will be given intensive care. 'It is important that these pioneering attempts are identified as doing research,' he says.

In some cases, it is simply not possible to treat very premature babies, he explains. 'For example, the trachea might be too narrow to insert a tube into.' In other cases, the controversial decision will have to be made by doctors in consultation with the parents, who in most cases should have the final say on whether treatment is withdrawn from their child, the panel agrees.

Decisions like these are set to become more frequent, since fertility treatment increases the number of multiple births – a risk factor for premature birth – and improvements to intensive care techniques save the lives of more babies that would previously have died.

Best practice

UK doctors greeted the report with mixed feelings. While some welcomed the guidelines, Tony Calland, chair of the medical ethics committee of the British Medical Association (BMA), says much of the report echoes 'existing best practice'.

But he says he disagrees with stringent cut-off points for treatment. 'The BMA believes that blanket rules do not help individual parents or their very premature babies,' he says. 'Each case should be considered on its merits and in its own context. While we believe that not all patients, including babies, benefit from medical intervention if survival is unlikely, it is important that each patient's circumstances are assessed independently.'

The UK has the highest rate of low birthweight babies in western Europe. The issue has been dealt with in different ways in other countries. In the Netherlands, severely disabled babies with low chance of survival may be legally euthanised.

In the US, as in the UK, euthanasia is not permitted, but some premature babies are allowed to die naturally. Many US doctors fear litigation and so are more reluctant to withdraw treatment than in the UK, Whitelaw notes. *15 November 2006*

⇨ Information from the *New Scientist*. Visit www.newscientist.com for more information.

© *New Scientist*

Happy end

By Yvonne Roberts

Neonatal consultant Michael Munro, cleared of misconduct in hastening the death of two terminally ill babies, has called for more debate on end-of-life decisions – but the debate has already continued for too long. What's required now is action.

Those who believe ending life is only a God-given right shouldn't be able to impede others who would prefer, in certain circumstances, to opt out

---

Dr Munro had administered a muscle relaxant, outside accepted professional practice, with the parents' permission. He did so when the babies suffered violent body spasms accompanied by irregular gasping breaths shortly before death.

The consultant had been accused of 'actions tantamount to euthanasia'. The failure of the Assisted Dying for the Terminally Ill Bill (ADTI bill) over a year ago – and the debate that it provoked revealed both the hypocrisy and the strength of the taboo around the business of dying.

The charity Dignity in Dying is planning another attempt to change the law (lost by 148 votes to 100 in the House of Lords) – but next time around instead of offering assisted dying only, the legislation should also include the option of voluntary euthanasia.

Those who believe ending life is only a God-given right shouldn't be able to impede others who would prefer, in certain circumstances, to opt out – for their own sakes and for the sakes of those around them.

The ADTI bill was so conservative that any fears its passing would lead to a 'slippery slope' of easy homicide should have been allayed. It had over 20 safeguards for the vulnerable including assessments by two independent doctors to establish whether the request to die is well informed and the need for the patient to make two oral and one written requests for assistance in dying.

Under the bill, in order to receive medical help to die, a person had to be adult, have less than six months to live with a terminal illness, be mentally competent, be suffering unbearably and had made persistent well-informed voluntary requests to die. Not much dignity in all that. Why not make the rules far easier?

Why, for instance, must doctors be involved? Why do you have to be terminally ill – why not include utterly debilitating but not terminal diseases? Why are you only allowed to request assisted dying in the last six months of life?

In Oregon, the Death with Dignity Act is 10 years old and similar to the ADTI bill in the UK. Less than 300 people have opted to end their lives. Numbers might have been higher, perhaps, if the rules were less stringent. However, the existence of the act has also helped to ensure high-quality hospice and palliative care – still desperately under-funded in the UK.

Good endings aren't easily acquired but signing a living will might help while having the option, in law, to choose your own departure date has to be an improvement on enduring what so often amounts to a living death.

12 July 2007

© *Guardian Newspapers Limited 2007*

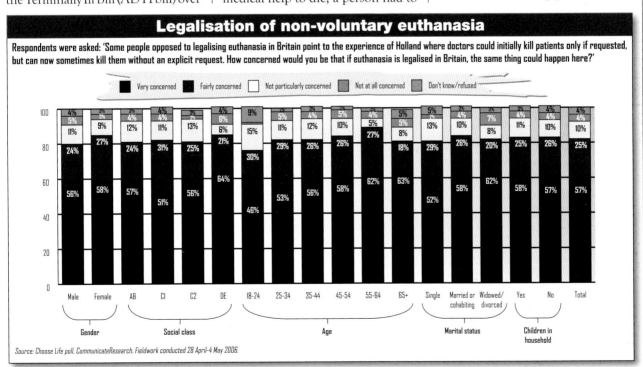

Legalisation of non-voluntary euthanasia

Respondents were asked: 'Some people opposed to legalising euthanasia in Britain point to the experience of Holland where doctors could initially kill patients only if requested, but can now sometimes kill them without an explicit request. How concerned would you be that if euthanasia is legalised in Britain, the same thing could happen here?'

Source: Choose Life poll, CommunicateResearch. Fieldwork conducted 28 April-4 May 2006.

Treatment for premature babies

Withdrawal and withholding treatment is sometimes appropriate, says CMF

The Christian Medical Fellowship has said that it is essential to understand the clear distinction between euthanasia and the appropriate withdrawal of ineffective and burdensome treatment from a dying baby.

It is essential to understand the clear distinction between euthanasia and the appropriate withdrawal of ineffective and burdensome treatment from a dying baby

CMF General Secretary Dr Peter Saunders said, 'On the one hand, actively and deliberately ending a baby's life is both wrong and illegal. On the other hand, withdrawing or withholding ineffective and burdensome treatment from a dying baby in extreme circumstances is both legal and ethical and can be good medical practice.'

CMF was responding to a report in the *Observer* and *Sunday Times*, which had confused the issue and wrongly implied that the Church of England supported euthanasia. 'Let's be quite clear about this,' said Dr Saunders. 'The Church of England has not changed its position on euthanasia. It has always been opposed to euthanasia and still is. The media hype surrounding the church's stance on this issue simply results from some broadsheet journalists failing to understand the clear distinction between euthanasia, which is the deliberate ending of someone's life, and the withdrawal of ineffective and burdensome treatment from a dying baby.

'If it's an underlying condition that's causing the death and you're withholding the treatment because you believe that that treatment's ineffective, then to do so is both legally and morally permissible. There's a point in medicine where we have to say that enough is enough, and sometimes the treatment can be worse than the disease. But that's a far cry from taking action intentionally to bring about a patient's death – which is what euthanasia means.

'End-of-life decisions shouldn't be confused with ending-life decisions,' said Dr Saunders.

'All human beings are worthy of the utmost respect, empathy, compassionate care and protection from abuse or harm. The mark of a humane society is that it takes special care to look after the most vulnerable. But there are untreatable or lethal clinical conditions for which invasive medical technology cannot bring a cure, and where we must focus instead on providing the best palliative care available to a baby who is terminally ill. In these circumstances, withholding or withdrawing life-sustaining treatment can be the appropriate course of action for a doctor to take, and it is perfectly legal and ethical for him to do so. Instead we should be providing good palliative care – fluids, pain and symptom relief, love and affection.

'In making these decisions we need to recognise that the outcome for any individual fetus or neonate depends on a wide range of contingencies and uncertainties which cannot be quantified or predicted with any degree of accuracy. If there is any doubt, babies, unborn or newborn, must be given the benefit of that doubt.'

13 November 2006

⇨ The above information is reprinted with kind permission from the Christian Medical Fellowship. Visit www.cmf.org.uk for more information.

© *Christian Medical Fellowship*

Advance decisions, advance statements and living wills

Information from Age Concern

Introduction

When you are ill, you can usually discuss treatment options with your doctor and then jointly reach a decision about your future care.

However you may be admitted to hospital when unconscious or unable, on a temporary or permanent basis, to make your own decisions about your treatment or communicate your wishes. This may happen, for example, if you have a car accident or a stroke or develop dementia. To use the technical term – you would 'lack mental capacity' to make an informed decision and / or communicate your wishes. In such situations, doctors have a legal and ethical obligation to act in your best interests. One exception to this is if you have made an advance decision refusing treatment. If this decision is valid and applicable to the circumstances, medical professionals providing your care are bound to follow it.

The term 'living will' could be used to refer to either an advance decision or an advance statement. An advance decision is a decision to refuse treatment; an advance statement is any other decision about how you would like to be treated. Only an advance decision is legally binding, but an advance statement should be taken into account when deciding what is in your best interests.

What is an advance statement?

This is a general statement of your wishes and views. It allows you to state your preferences and indicate what treatment or care you would like to receive should you, in the future, be unable to decide or communicate your wishes for yourself. It can include non medical things such as your food beliefs or preferences or whether you would prefer a bath to a shower.

It could reflect your religious or other beliefs and any aspects of life which you particularly value.

It can help those involved in your care to know more about what is important to you. It must be considered by the people providing your treatment when they determine what is in your best interests, but they are not legally bound to follow your wishes.

Advance statements can also be used to let the people treating you know who you would like to be consulted at a time a decision has to be made, if you are unable to make that decision yourself.

If you create a Lasting Power of Attorney (LPA), you could record an advance statement in the LPA document. An LPA can be used if you want to give someone else, or more than one person, the power to make decisions about your care and treatment if you are not able to do so yourself. Your attorney(s) must take your advance statement into account when deciding what is in your best interests. See below for more information about LPAs.

What is an advance decision to refuse treatment?

An advance decision to refuse treatment is the only type of living will that is legally binding. An adult with mental capacity can refuse treatment for any reason, even if this might lead to their death. However no one is able to insist that a particular medical treatment is given, if it conflicts with what the medical professionals providing the treatment conclude is in the patient's best interests. This is why an advance decision can only be a refusal of treatment.

An advance decision to refuse treatment must indicate exactly what type of treatment you wish to refuse and should give as much detail as

necessary about the circumstances under which this refusal would apply. It is not necessary to use precise medical terms, as long as it is clear what treatment is to be refused in what circumstances.

An advance decision can only be made by someone over age 18 who has the mental capacity to make the decision. This means they must be able to understand, weigh up and retain the relevant information in order to make the decision to refuse treatment; and they are then able to communicate that decision.

How to make an advance decision to refuse treatment

An advance decision does not have to be in writing, unless it is a decision to refuse life-sustaining treatment (see the next section below for the legal requirements for this type of decision). Verbal instructions can amount to a valid advance decision but there is more risk that a verbal refusal of treatment would not be carried out. The person providing treatment may not be aware of it, or there could be uncertainty about its validity or applicability.

For example, a statement made by a patient during a discussion with their doctor that they would not wish to have a particular type of treatment in certain circumstances in the future can be a valid advance decision without it being put in writing. It would be best practice for the doctor to record the statement in the patient's medical records, but it can still be valid if this is not done. Even if you are putting your advance decision in writing yourself, it is a good idea to discuss it with your doctor.

To avoid uncertainty over the validity of an advance decision you should put it in writing, or ask someone else to write it down for you, if possible. It is helpful to use the following guidelines:

⇨ Put the decision in writing
⇨ Include your name, date of birth, address and details of your GP
⇨ Include a statement that you wish the advance decision to apply if you lack the capacity to make the decision yourself at the relevant time.
⇨ Specify what kind of treatment is to be refused and in what circumstances, giving as much detail as possible.
⇨ Sign and date the document.
⇨ Ask someone to witness your signature.

You could ask your doctor or another relevant professional to sign a statement on the document stating that they have carried out an assessment of you and, in their opinion, you have the mental capacity to make the decision.

Remember that the above points are not legal requirements, but they can help to avoid uncertainty over the validity and applicability of your advance decision. There are legal requirements if you are making an advance decision to refuse life-sustaining treatment. See below for details of these.

Why make an advance decision?

You may wish to make an advance decision if you have strong feelings about a particular situation that could arise in the future. This might relate to having a limb amputated following an accident or having a blood transfusion.

More commonly, you may have been told that you have a terminal illness or form of dementia. You may wish to prepare an advance decision indicating the type of treatment you would not want to receive in the future. Making an advance decision may give you peace of mind in knowing that your wishes should not be ignored if you are unable to take part in the decision making process at the relevant time.

Considering making an advance decision provides an opportunity to talk to and ask questions of your medical team during the early stages of an illness rather than delaying it until it is more difficult to participate. It can also provide an opportunity to discuss what may be difficult issues with family and friends.

You do not have to make an advance decision. You may decide to leave it to the healthcare professionals providing your treatment to decide what is in your best interests. When deciding this, they should take into account any evidence they have of your past wishes, your beliefs and values; and they should consult your friends, family and carers where appropriate. They may decide that what is in your best interests is not the same as what you would have decided to do yourself.

What an advance decision cannot be used for

An advance decision cannot be used to:

⇨ ask for anything that is illegal such as euthanasia or for help to commit suicide;
⇨ demand care the healthcare team considers inappropriate in your case;
⇨ refuse the offer of food and drink by mouth;
⇨ refuse the use of measures solely designed to maintain your comfort such as providing appropriate pain relief, warmth or shelter;
⇨ refuse basic nursing care that is essential to keep you comfortable such as washing, bathing and mouth care.

Who to consult about an advance decision

It is not necessary to involve a solicitor, although you may wish a solicitor to confirm that your views are clearly presented in the document.

It is always advisable to discuss your intentions with a medical professional such as your GP and your family and friends.

If you have a terminal illness, you may wish to speak to the doctor involved in your care. He/she can help you understand the consequences of refusing or opting for a particular treatment and relate specific decisions to the likely course of your illness. This doctor can also help you express your wishes clearly and verify you were competent at the time you prepared and signed the document.

October 2007

⇨ Age Concern publishes a range of information on issues of importance to older people. For more information on this topic or to order other materials visit the Age Concern website at www.ageconcern.co.uk/information or call our information line free on 0800 00 99 66.

Advance decisions and the Mental Capacity Act

This article answers frequently asked questions about advance decisions (formerly known as living wills) and the Mental Capacity Act

What is the Mental Capacity Act?

The Mental Capacity Act is new Government legislation which provides a statutory framework to empower and protect vulnerable people who are not able to make their own decisions.

It achieves this, in part, by enabling people to plan ahead for a time when they may lose capacity. The aspects which involve planning ahead, namely advance decisions and Lasting Powers of Attorney, come into force on 1st October 2007.

What changes have been made to advance decisions/ living wills?

The same rules apply to advance decisions as did to our previous living will. The main difference is that under the Mental Capacity Act if you wish to refuse life-sustaining treatment you must include a statement saying that this is your will, even if the result will be the shortening of your life. This statement is included in Dignity in Dying's new advance decision.

The Mental Capacity Act guidance states that the situations set out in the advance decision must be unambiguous. This means that you should be as clear and specific as you can. This is why our new advance decision includes a section where you can add, in your own words, exactly the situations in which you would

Dignity
in dying
your life, your choice

like to refuse or consent to treatment (sections 1 (D) and 2 (C)).

We also continue to strongly advise that you talk to your GP about your advance decision.

Is my existing living will legally binding?

The Mental Capacity Act states that 'The advance decision must include a clear, specific written statement from the person making the advance decision that the advance decision is to apply to the specific treatment even if life is at risk.'

You can continue to use your existing advance decision/living will, but in order to ensure that it is legally binding under the MCA you must write the following statement in the section referring to the refusal of life-sustaining treatment:

'The decisions set out in my living will apply, even if my life is at risk as a result.'

You need to sign and date this statement, and get it witnessed.

Do I have to amend every copy?

You can amend your personal copy and send a photocopy of the amendment to the people you have lodged your advance decision/living will with, e.g. your GP, friend, relative or solicitor, and ask them to attach it to their copy of your living will.

Your original copy may be called upon should your living will need to be used, so do ensure that someone else knows where it is kept.

How frequently should I review my advance decision/ living will?

This is a question that we are regularly asked and unfortunately is impossible for us to answer, as there has been no guidance provided in the Mental Capacity Act. Our advice is to review and re-sign it regularly and ensure you re-sign it if you know you are being admitted into hospital.

How will my treating health care team know I have an advance decision?

The ongoing problem here is that there will still be no registration facility for advance decisions and therefore it is the responsibility of the individual to show that they have one. You can do this by carrying your 'notice of advance decision card' (which comes with the new Dignity in Dying advance decision), or carrying a copy of your advance decision with you.

This is why Dignity in Dying's living wills registration campaign is so important. Please sign up to our campaign to ensure that your end-of-life wishes, as set out in your advance decision, are respected.

⇨ The above information is reprinted with kind permission from Dignity in Dying. Visit www.dignityindying.org.uk for more information.

© Dignity in Dying

Doctors get right over life or death

Doctors have been given the legal right to let their patients die for the first time.

The new Mental Capacity Act yesterday established a doctor's right to take the decision that providing life-saving treatment is futile if there is no prospect of recovery.

Doctors have been given the legal right to let their patients die for the first time

Powers to end life will also go to other people such as lawyers, social workers, friends or relatives if they have been nominated in advance by the patient as someone with the right to take life-or-death decisions.

Doctors have been entitled to let patients die by withdrawing treatment – usually food and water for a tube-fed patient – for 14 years under a House of Lords precedent.

By Steve Doughty, Social Affairs Correspondent

And since 1999 the British Medical Association has said that it can be in a patient's best interests to die.

But the new legislation sets down the right to end life in statute law.

Critics said the Act would let doctors kill patients who are not dying.

Phyllis Bowman, of the Right to Life group, said: 'The Government have always said withdrawal of life-sustaining treatment would not be "enshrined in statute law". That is now exactly what they have done.

'The trick is the phrase about "no prospect of recovery". I have no prospect of recovery from my asthma, but that doesn't mean I want to be killed. The same applies to people who are incapacitated and cannot speak for themselves.'

The law states: 'There will be a limited number of cases where treatment is futile, overly burdensome to the patients or where there is no prospect of recovery.

'It may be that an assessment leads to the conclusion that it would be in the best interests of the patient to withdraw or withhold life-sustaining treatment, even if this may result in the person's death.'

But it adds that the decision to let a patient die 'must not be motivated by a desire to bring about a person's death for whatever reason, even if this is from a sense of compassion'.

The Mental Capacity Act, squeezed through Parliament in 2005 despite a rebellion by Labour backbenchers, has been condemned by critics for allowing 'back-door euthanasia'.

It allows people to make living wills in which they can stipulate that they should be allowed to die if they become incapacitated and dependent on medical treatment to stay alive. Treatment, legally, includes provision of food and water by tube.

A new branch of the High Court, the Court of Protection, will be set up to deal with arguments over how patients should be treated.

⇨ This article first appeared in the *Daily Mail*, 23 February 2007.

© 2007 Associated Newspapers Ltd

Can computers make life-or-death medical decisions?

Information from the *New Scientist*

By Roxanne Khamsi

A simple formula can predict how people would want to be treated in dire medical situations as accurately as their loved ones can, say researchers.

The finding suggests that computers may one day help doctors and those acting as surrogate decision-makers to better estimate the wishes of people in a coma.

By signing what is known as an 'advance directive', people can specify what types of medical care they would want if they lost the ability to make decisions. Many people, however, do not complete such a directive in advance of these critical situations and their relatives or others must then decide on their behalf.

But how well can surrogates accurately predict the wishes of patients? Researchers have previously addressed this question by asking people how they would want to be treated in various hypothetical medical scenarios and, in a separate room, asking surrogates to guess what those responses had been. A review of 16 studies found that surrogates got it right only 68% of the time.

Reason and remember

Bioethicist David Wendler of

the National Institutes of Health in Bethesda, Maryland, US, and colleagues wondered whether a formula could be used to better predict a patient's wishes. They examined information collected by pollsters and scientists about the attitudes towards medical care held by the general US population.

The data suggested that most people want life-saving treatment if there is at least a 1% chance that following the intervention they would have the ability to reason, remember and communicate. If there is less than a 1% chance, people generally say they would choose not to have the treatment.

A simple formula can predict how people would want to be treated in dire medical situations as accurately as their loved ones can, say researchers

---

'The difference between zero and 1% is all the difference in the world for someone,' says Wendler.

Surprising accuracy

His team then looked at a subset of the 16 studies in which the medical scenarios were judged to be easier for a member of the public to understand. In these cases, they found that surrogates predicted the patient's wishes more accurately, 78% of the time. But surprisingly, using the formula that people only want interventions if there is a 1% chance of a good outcome had the same accuracy.

Wendler says he was surprised at the formula's accuracy. 'I think it's fascinating. At first when you hear it you think "That just can't be right,"' he says.

He imagines a situation in which a surrogate is told there is only a 5% chance that an incapacitated loved one will survive a life-saving surgery following an auto accident. He says that the relative might predict that

the patient would not want the intervention while the formula would predict that they did.

Wendler now wants to collect medical care preferences from people of various ethnic, religious and gender groups, which will help his team refine the formula. He believes that a computer program might one day predict patient's wishes to an accuracy of 90%.

And the tool could take some of the pressure off of relatives who sometimes have to decide whether or not to switch off a patient's life-support machine.

Question of ethics

However, critics caution that computer algorithms should never supplant human surrogates. 'I believe it would be extremely irresponsible to allow machines to make decisions involving life and death,' says Bobby Schindler, brother of Terri Schiavo.

Schiavo was in a persistent vegetative state for 15 years until she died in 2005 after doctors removed her feeding tube. Her case sparked huge debate in the US.

'If a person becomes incapacitated, is not dying, and can assimilate food and water via a feeding tube, then I believe that we are morally obligated to care for the person and provide them this basic care – regardless of a computer attempting to "predict" what that person's wishes might be,' Schindler adds.

'Essentially, you would be allowing a machine to determine what is ethical, what is right and wrong, which no machine is able to do.'
13 March 2007

⇨ The above information is reprinted with kind permission from the *New Scientist*. Visit www.newscientist.com for more information.

© *New Scientist*

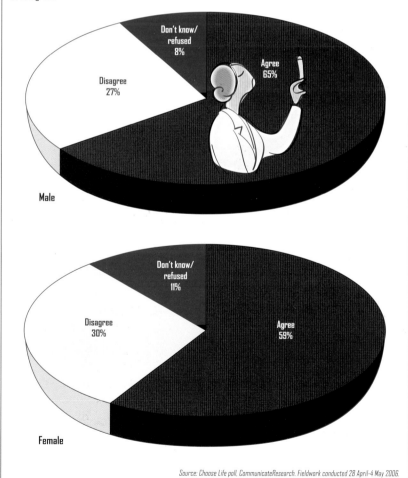

Attractiveness of euthanasia to the elderly

Respondents were asked: 'Some suggest a link between the poor quality of social care towards the end of life, and the attractiveness to some elderly people of euthanasia and doctor-assisted suicide. Do you tend to agree or disagree?'

Male
- Don't know/refused 8%
- Disagree 27%
- Agree 65%

Female
- Don't know/refused 11%
- Disagree 30%
- Agree 59%

Source: Choose Life poll, CommunicateResearch. Fieldwork conducted 28 April-4 May 2006.

⇨ Euthanasia is against the law in the UK. It is illegal to aid someone to take their life under any circumstances. 'Assisted suicide' or voluntary euthanasia can result in a prison sentence of up to 14 years. (page 1)

⇨ The World Medical Association (WMA) declared euthanasia unethical in 1950. (page 1)

⇨ 72% of 18- to 24-year-olds polled by Communicate Research agreed that the vulnerable could feel under pressure to opt for suicide if euthanasia were made legal. (page 2)

⇨ It is generally accepted that as an expression of autonomy, i.e. one's right to make independent choices without any external influences, a competent adult can refuse medical treatment, even in situations where this could result in his/her death. (page 3)

⇨ There are fears that allowing euthanasia would encourage the practice to become the norm, as it might be easier and cheaper to provide than other forms of end-of-life healthcare. (page 4)

⇨ Some people distinguish 'active' euthanasia – administering a lethal injection – from 'passive' euthanasia – withholding or withdrawing treatment. (page 5)

⇨ 73% of those in the over 50 age group polled by YouGov agreed that assisted dying for the terminally ill should be legal, compared with 81% of those aged 30 to 50 and 72% of 18- to 29-year-olds. (page 11)

⇨ 76% of respondents in a YouGov survey either agreed or strongly agreed that terminally ill people should be allowed medical assistance to die. 56% agreed or strongly agreed that those with a non-terminal but incurable illness should also be allowed medical help to die upon request. (page 12)

⇨ 80 British citizens have travelled to Dignitas in Switzerland to end their lives. (page 15)

⇨ 78% of 55- to 64-year-olds surveyed by Communicate Research felt that legalising physician assisted suicide would make it more difficult to detect rogue doctors like Harold Shipman. (page 18)

⇨ Legislation allowing assisted suicide, however tight the controls, inevitably reinforces negative attitudes on the quality of life of disabled people. (page 20)

⇨ Palliative care and assisted dying are often presented as opposing forces. Some critics of assisted dying state that legislating for assisted dying could undermine developments to palliative care. (page 22)

⇨ A new survey finds British doctors used euthanasia to kill nearly 3,000 patients in 2004. The poll also found that British doctors do not want to see the legalisation of assisted suicide despite a campaign to do that. (page 23)

⇨ The British Medical Association voted in its 2005 annual meeting to drop its resistance to a change in the law on assisted suicide and adopt a stance of neutrality, making it a matter for society to decide. (page 25)

⇨ More than half of GPs have withheld treatment from terminally ill patients knowing it could hasten death, a survey by *Pulse* magazine suggested. (page 25)

⇨ Morphine is a safe and effective painkiller and should never cause death, according to a major new study which explodes the myth that doctors use the drug to hasten the end for terminally ill patients. (page 26)

⇨ A study of doctor-assisted suicide in the Netherlands and Oregon counters the argument that making it legal may lead to more of these deaths among vulnerable groups like the disabled, although it did find some evidence for this among people with AIDS. (page 31)

⇨ About 80 per cent of those who died with a doctor's help in the Netherlands and Oregon were cancer patients. (page 31)

⇨ The Mental Capacity Act is new Government legislation which provides a statutory framework to empower and protect vulnerable people who are not able to make their own decisions. It achieves this, in part, by enabling people to plan ahead for a time when they may lose capacity. The aspects which involve planning ahead, namely advance decisions and Lasting Powers of Attorney, come into force on 1st October 2007. (page 37)

⇨ A simple formula can predict how people would want to be treated in dire medical situations as accurately as their loved ones can, say researchers. The finding suggests that computers may one day help doctors and those acting as surrogate decision-makers to better estimate the wishes of people in a coma. (page 38)

⇨ 65% of men surveyed by Communicate Research agreed that there is likely to be a link between poor quality of social care towards the end of life and the attractiveness to some elderly people of euthanasia and doctor assisted suicide. This compares with 59% of women who agreed. (page 39)

GLOSSARY

Advance directive
Advance directives, sometimes referred to as 'living wills', are written statements outlining a person's wishes concerning the type of medical treatment they would like to receive should they fall ill and be unable to make medical decisions. Doctors and health workers are required by law to take advance directives into account when treating a patient.

Assisted suicide
Assisting a person to commit suicide by providing the means for them to take their own life. Physician-assisted suicide (PAS) is when lethal drugs are prescribed by a doctor but administered by the patient. Assisted suicide is legal in the Netherlands, Switzerland and the state of Oregon in the United States.

Autonomy
A person's ability and power to make their own decisions, independent of outside influences. Some people argue that patients should have greater autonomy over their own medical treatment and the freedom to choose euthanasia if they wish.

'Death tourism'
Dubbed 'death' or 'suicide tourism', this refers to someone with a desire to die travelling to another country – in the UK, this is usually Switzerland – in order to legally end their life.

Do-Not-Resuscitate Order (DNR)
A written order stating that should a patient suffer cardiac or respiratory arrest, no attempt should be made to revive them – they should be allowed to die. This is not considered euthanasia and is legal in the UK. The order may be based on an advance directive.

Double effect
The doctrine or principle of double effect is applied when the treatment a doctor prescribes to relieve a patient's pain has the additional result of ending their life. The doctor may be aware that the drugs will quicken the patient's death, but the intention is to ease their pain rather than to cause death – thus, as the intention is pain relief and death is brought about only as a side-effect of this, this is not considered to be euthanasia. It would only result in the prosecution of a doctor if there was doubt as to their true intention in prescribing the medicine.

Euthanasia
Intentionally ending the life of somebody for what may be seen as compassionate reasons. The word 'euthanasia' comes from a Greek term meaning 'good death'. It is sometimes referred to as 'mercy killing' as it can bring a painless end to a person's suffering, such as a terminally ill person, or to someone who has little or no quality of life. Euthanasia is against the law in the UK but has been legalised, under certain conditions, in the Netherlands and Belgium. It is a highly contentious topic in the UK, provoking much debate among both religious and non-religious people.

Hospice
A programme of palliative care and support for terminally ill patients reaching the end of their lives, as well as their families.

Involuntary euthanasia
Ending the life of a patient who has not requested or consented for their life to be ended.

Palliative care
Medical treatment or care that reduces the suffering of a terminally ill patient but does not provide a cure for their illness. The purpose of the treatment is to relieve pain and improve the quality of life of the patient. Some people argue that if good-quality palliative care were made available to patients, then they would not feel the need to resort to euthanasia.

Passive euthanasia
Not directly ending a person's life, but allowing them to die by withholding or withdrawing treatment necessary to prolong their life – for example, turning off a life-support machine.

Non-voluntary euthanasia
Ending the life of a patient who is not able or competent to request euthanasia.

Sanctity of life
The idea within Christianity and other religions that all life is sacred as it has been created by God. This term is often used in debates surrounding issues such as euthanasia and abortion.

Terminal illness
An illness for which there is no known cure and therefore no chance of recovery.

Persistent vegetative state (PVS)
A persistent vegetative state is a coma-like state in which the patient may experience periods of wakefulness, yet has no awareness of themselves or their surroundings.

Voluntary euthanasia
Ending the life of a patient who has requested and given consent for their life to be ended.

INDEX

Additional Resources

Other Issues *titles*

If you are interested in researching further some of the issues raised in *Euthanasia and the Right to Die*, you may like to read the following titles in the **Issues** series:

➪ Vol. 148 *Religious Beliefs* (ISBN 978 1 86168 421 9)

➪ Vol. 144 *The Cloning Debate* (ISBN 978 1 86168 410 3)

➪ Vol. 136 *Self-Harm* (ISBN 978 1 86168 388 5)

➪ Vol. 135 *Coping with Disability* (ISBN 978 1 86168 387 8)

➪ Vol. 126 *The Abortion Debate* (ISBN 978 1 86168 365 6)

➪ Vol. 125 *Understanding Depression* (ISBN 978 1 86168 364 9)

➪ Vol. 120 *The Human Rights Issue* (ISBN 978 1 86168 353 3)

➪ Vol. 116 *Grief and Loss* (ISBN 978 1 86168 349 6)

➪ Vol. 105 *Ageing Issues* (ISBN 978 1 86168 325 0)

➪ Vol. 81 *Alternative Therapies* (ISBN 978 1 86168 276 5)

➪ Vol. 60 *Confronting Cancer* (ISBN 978 1 86168 230 7)

For more information about these titles, visit our website at www.independence.co.uk/publicationslist

Useful organisations

You may find the websites of the following organisations useful for further research:

➪ **Age Concern:** www.ageconcern.org.uk

➪ **Australian Voluntary Euthanasia Society:** www.saves.asn.au

➪ **Care NOT Killing:** www.carenotkilling.org.uk

➪ **Christian Medical Fellowship:** www.cmf.org.uk

➪ **Dignity in Dying:** www.dignityindying.org.uk

➪ **Disability Awareness in Action:** www.daa.org.uk

➪ **Irish Council for Bioethics:** www.bioethics.ie

➪ **LifeNews:** www.lifenews.com

➪ **The New Scientist:** www.newscientist.com

➪ **NHS Direct:** www.nhsdirect.nhs.uk

➪ **Nursing Standard:** www.nursing-standard.co.uk

➪ **Religious Tolerance:** www.religioustolerance.org

➪ **Reuters:** www.reuters.com

➪ **The Royal Society:** http://royalsociety.org

➪ **YouGov:** www.yougov.com

ACKNOWLEDGEMENTS

The publisher is grateful for permission to reproduce the following material.

While every care has been taken to trace and acknowledge copyright, the publisher tenders its apology for any accidental infringement or where copyright has proved untraceable. The publisher would be pleased to come to a suitable arrangement in any such case with the rightful owner.

Chapter One: The Ethical Debate

Euthanasia, © Crown copyright is reproduced with the permission of Her Majesty's Stationery Office, Your body, your death, your choice?, © Irish Council for Bioethics, Euthanasia and assisted suicide, © Care NOT Killing, We must help people die with dignity, © The Argus, Answering the euthanasia critics, © Australian Voluntary Euthanasia Society, A dubious distinction, © Guardian Newspapers Ltd, Public opinion on assisted dying, © Dignity in Dying, What do the public think?, © Care NOT Killing, Euthanasia: 'we should not be made to suffer like this', © Telegraph Group Ltd, Euthanasia: the legal issues, © Nursing Standard, Legal status of euthanasia around the world, © Reuters, Assisted suicide and disabled people, © Disability Awareness in Action, Fury as euthanasia group puts dignity in new name, © Telegraph Group Ltd, Palliative care, © Dignity in Dying.

Chapter Two: The Medical Debate

How common is euthanasia?, © LifeNews.com, Euthanasia: a doctor's viewpoint, © Brunel University, West London, Majority of GPs 'stop treating terminally ill', © Telegraph Group Ltd, Morphine kills pain not patients, © Care NOT Killing, Should we legalise euthanasia?, © Associated Newspapers Ltd, Call for euthanasia legislation, © Royal Society, Physician-assisted suicide, © Ontario Consultants on Religious Tolerance, Study counters argument against assisted suicide, © Reuters, When premature babies should be allowed to die, © New Scientist, Happy end, © Guardian Newspapers Ltd, Treatment for premature babies, © Christian Medical Fellowship, Advance decisions, advance statements and living wills, © Age Concern, Advance decisions and the Mental Capacity Act, © Dignity in Dying, Doctors get right over life or death, © Associated Newspapers Ltd, Can computers make life-or-death medical decisions?, © New Scientist.

Photographs

Flickr: pages 20 (neovain); 21 (Tim Samoff).
Stock Xchng: pages 5 (Iwan Beijes); 7 (Melodi T); 13 (Gary Scott); 27, 28 (Adam Ciesielski); 35 (tulp).
Wikimedia: pages 16 (Woudloper); 37 (S Sepp).

Illustrations

Pages 1, 19, 24, 34: Simon Kneebone; pages 6, 17: Bev Aisbett; pages 12, 22, 25, 36: Don Hatcher; pages 15, 23, 29, 31: Angelo Madrid.

Research and glossary by Claire Owen, with additional by Lisa Firth, on behalf of Independence Educational Publishers.

Additional editorial by Claire Owen, on behalf of Independence Educational Publishers.

And with thanks to the team: Mary Chapman, Sandra Dennis, Claire Owen and Jan Sunderland.

Lisa Firth
Cambridge
April, 2008